WHITE COLLAR WASTE:

GAIN THE PRODUCTIVITY EDGE

VAL OLSON

Prentice-Hall, Inc.
Englewood Cliffs, N.J. 07632

Δ

Table of Contents

Acknowledgments

I should like to express my gratitude and thanks to the following friends and colleagues, without whose help this book would not have been possible.

Robert Worden, Ronald Wight, and Thomas Zavadsky are responsible for breathing life into many of the procedures described in the text. Robert Pawlik and Roberto Cordero provided invaluable insights and advice on productivity measurement in chapter four.

Special thanks goes to my CMA℠ colleague, Roberto Cordero, for developing a strategic planning model based on our measurement methodology. The book argues that productivity measurement is the foundation upon which a white collar productivity improvement program must be built and is, potentially, the key ingredient of a total blueprint for management. This position is demonstrated by Mr. Cordero in appendix one, and I am particularly grateful for this work.

Finally, a special acknowledgment should go to Bazil J. van Loggerenberg and to the American Productivity Center for their work in the field of productivity measurement.

Preface

In the first chapter of *White Collar Waste,* I refer to the book as a long overdue manifesto on white collar productivity. It is just that. And more. It is a call to American management to get involved, to return to the logic of basic management skills. It is an opening presentation of a new, aggressive management posture of the future.

Let me explain that last statement. Common competitors have common markets. They must be able to compete in the arenas of price, service, and quality. When they assemble their input elements (expenses), they encounter general similarity in cost and inflation considerations. As a result, business expenses are viewed as benign ingredients that must be tolerated in the quest for market share, growth, and profits. Such a view is only practical when all competitors share a common passthrough expense mentality.

Then, in what camp is the battle joined? In these terms, the battle is joined in the marketing/sales camp.

Such was the state of the art until the foreign hordes came with their steel, cameras, cars, and televisions. They had broken ranks and started managing their input elements. Now the battle is joined in the expense camp. Marketing cannot overcome high prices and questionable quality. We have been brought back to reality. Not a passing phenomenon but one we will live with in perpetuity. The passthrough mentality of the past several decades was the passing phenomenon.

This, then, is the "opening presentation of a new, aggressive management posture of the future." Our input elements are not lifeless, one-dimensional expense considerations. Expenses are multidimensional. Expenses have a capacity for a range of utilization. Optimizing that range is the stuff of future management. Productivity analysis is the critical management tool of the future.

In this book, I deal with these issues in general and with the major white collar expense issue—people—in particular. People as a productivity issue are analyzed into manageable principles. The principles are then assembled into workable solutions.

This is, in effect, a manifesto on white collar productivity.

Management and Labor

In 1981, Sentry Insurance Company sponsored a study conducted by Louis Harris, Inc., entitled, *Perspectives on Productivity: A Global View (1981).*[1] The study was described as "the most comprehensive international public opinion survey ever conducted on the subject of productivity." The portions of the study especially intriguing are those on the American public's understanding of productivity and related problems. I can speak glibly about white collar productivity being a management issue that is amenable to durable solutions; but, what about the public, the worker? Are not management and labor adversaries?

It wasn't too long ago that "efficiency" and "productivity" were considered unpleasant words by the average American worker. This attitude is epitomized by a scene from a movie classic, Charlie Chaplin's *Modern Times,* a scene that left its mark on a generation of workers. Charlie is working on an assembly line with a wrench, tightening bolts on widgets as they pass before him. Management gradually speeds up the line and Charlie, in turn, steps up his pace. Before long, he is jumping around frantically to keep up with the objects flashing by on the line.

That scene set the tone for the public's opinion on worker productivity. Starting in the early 1900's, the American public equated productivity improvement with management speeding up the line, driving workers to perform their jobs faster and faster. Charlie's frantic scurrying in the film typified the attitude of confrontation that has characterized labor-management relations for so many years. Now we can see, with the benefit of hindsight, that there were wrongs on both sides. And it is this realization that is changing the old, adversarial roles of management and labor. Today, both sides are mellowing.

The Harris study documents this attitude change. Labor's attitude is important. Though American management is the productivity problem, we must solve that problem through the instrumentality of the worker. If you seek evidence of this

---

[1] See appendix two for a summary.

3

management/worker relationship, note that white collar labor contracts are now dealing with management's methodology for enhancing productivity.

White collar productivity is a labor contract subject because of the machine mentality that undergirds the blue collar approach to low productivity. Most white collar productivity improvement programs find their origins in blue collar industries. Throughout this text, I make the point that we must address the issue of white collar productivity on its own merits; that white collar productivity is a science rooted in its own principles and developing at a different evolutionary pace from blue collar productivity.

Though I expose white collar waste on a unit, division, and company basis, white collar waste is also an urgent national issue. After all, the whole is the sum of the parts, and in this instance, the parts form a startling whole.

The 4/8 Theory

American white collar employees today on average produce only four hours of effective work out of each eight-hour workday.

Farfetched as it may seem initially, this 4/8 Theory has been substantiated through almost two decades of my experience in the field of white collar productivity, involving hundreds of offices across the country. Although the figures vary somewhat from case to case, the evidence indicates that the typical U.S. office worker is now functioning at only 50 percent of maximum potential efficiency.

On a national scale, the implications of the 4/8 Theory are truly staggering. White collar workers presently account for more than half of the total American work force—some 50 million workers in all. The awful truth is that the U.S. economy is paying for billions upon billions of wasted work-hours every year.

4

How has this monumental problem of white collar waste remained hidden from public view? Part of the answer is that, until now, America's productivity dilemma has been diagnosed exclusively as a blue collar ailment. National attention has focused on the impact of unfavorable productivity trends in the manufacturing sector of the U.S. economy. The devastation of such industries as autos and steel, basic to the American way of life, has captured the headlines.

But the main reason the issue of white collar waste has gone unnoticed is that American corporate managers, with few exceptions, do not even suspect the problem exists. American companies have thrown billions of investment dollars into computers, word processing systems, and similar sophisticated equipment in an effort to upgrade office productivity. Yet management has totally overlooked the most basic factor of all—the process of office work itself. When white collar work is subject to scientific scrutiny, it quickly becomes evident that office productivity differs fundamentally from blue collar productivity. Blue collar productivity is closely related to machines and is determined by rate of activity. White collar productivity, as defined by the 4/8 Theory, does not depend on how fast an office employee works; it hinges, rather, on the *efficient use of time.*

An Urgent National Problem

The 4/8 Theory says quite clearly that *the white collar segment of our American work force is overstaffed—overstaffed to the tune of millions of workers.* To put the figure into better perspective, the average American white collar worker represents an annual cost of $20,000. (This is a conservative figure that includes salary, benefits, furniture, and floor space. Many workers cost much less than that figure; but, on the other hand, most engineers, accountants, managers, and lawyers cost more than that in salary alone.) Using a figure of $20,000, every million white collar workers carries an annual $20 billion price tag for

5

American business. And, remember, we are overstaffed by millions of workers. The only way American business and industry will survive figures of that magnitude is to employ those millions of workers productively.

It is strange that this point is not being emphasized by today's economists. The white collar industries are people-intensive. If these industries face a serious productivity problem, then we as a nation have a serious overstaffing problem. There are only so many juxtapositions of those two issues. We are not going to solve a productivity problem of this magnitude without initially disrupting jobs. In fact, we have only three options if we intend to solve it at all. The first solution is the desirable one.

Three Solutions

1) The first is to keep our work force constant while increasing production to utilize its capacity. This is a practical approach for individual companies because they can take production from weaker competitors and pass the overstaffing problem on to them. The question is, how do you do that with an entire nation? The answer is to do at the national level what companies do. And the Catch 22 is the same: you must first become a success compared with your international competitors. To become successful takes us to the second solution.

2) The second solution is the emotionally tough one of controlling input. For your output to grow, compared with that of an efficient competitor, your expenses and therefore productivity must be competitive. In white collar industries, the controllable input element is people. Now we are back to our original dilemma, however—the initial disruption of jobs.

3) A third solution is to increase output while bringing input under control. This is undoubtedly the course the solution ultimately will take. Therefore, we will never be able to quantify accurately the disruption of jobs. Simply understand

6

that if we are to work at enhancing the parts, we must be aware of the effect on the whole.

The good news is that, as we reduce our expenses by billions of dollars, we improve our international marketing position. With high national productivity come moderated prices and expanded overseas markets as well as recovery of our domestic markets. And that, in the end, means jobs.

2

White Collar Productivity: The Theory

Today, it is popular to approach white collar productivity problems with a series of remedies. Get into a discussion on the subject, and no one will talk about the underlying causes of America's productivity headache. Instead, the conversation will be restricted to the popular brands of aspirin that are available.

We all know the brands:

- Quality-of-Work-Life
- Quality Circles
- Suggestion Systems
- Employee Measurement Systems
- Mechanization/Computerization
- Participative Management
- Monetary Reward Systems
- Etc.

If you're talking with a white collar productivity expert, ask that individual to talk about the subject without mentioning one of the above aspirin brands. The ensuing silence will be deafening.

In this chapter, I discuss both the root causes of the headache and its remedies. In chapters six, seven, and eight, I explain the remedy that best matches the white collar industry's available managerial resources with the problem. In chapter five, I briefly describe the other remedies being offered today, so that you can view the entire white collar productivity issue from the broadest possible perspective.

You may better understand the conclusions regarding white collar productivity if I relate how I developed them. In the mid-1960's I worked with a management consulting firm specializing in white collar and blue collar efficiency. This was a very intense and interesting experience. It gave me the opportunity to evaluate various productivity enhancement methods and determine their strengths and weaknesses. The firm had fixed ideas about what techniques and procedures were necessary to improve a client company's efficiency. The firm never instructed me in logic or theory.

Over the years, I have had opportunities to evaluate the activities of many large consulting firms from the client's vantage point. Again and again, they suggested techniques and procedures but never provided a fundamental explanation of the productivity theory or logic they used. I can only assume that the fundamentals of white collar managerial theory are not widely recognized.

In the sixties, I was exposed for the first time to a basic theory that I believe goes to the very heart of the white collar productivity issue. At that time, the theory was not defined in depth and did not have a name. As stated in chapter one, the implications of the theory are too profound for it to remain nameless.

I call it the 4/8 Theory.

Simply put, the theory maintains that the average white collar employee returns four effective hours of work effort for every eight hours of work for which the employer pays. I cannot remember in what specific context I initially heard this statement, but I do recall that it was a passing comment, not a substantive issue that was being raised. You often hear or read the same comment today, usually as a revelation being disclosed for the first time, but never fleshed out in any detail. To deal effectively with the white collar productivity issue, we have to secure a foundation of conventional, manageable wisdom. Armed with basic, dependable knowledge, we can prepare to attack the productivity problem. With the 4/8 Theory we begin this process.

Initially, I greeted the 4/8 Theory with disbelief and, I admit, ridicule. After all, most of us started on the lower rungs of the white collar ladder. We didn't waste half our workday. As managers, we lived eight hours a day in the workplace with our employees, and those individuals obviously were not wasting half of their workdays. Indeed, what kind of managers would condone such blatant waste?

The 4/8 Theory is much more subtle. It is subtle because there is nothing naturally demonstrable about it, nor is it founded on the intent of the white collar employee. I was gradually won over to the 4/8 Theory as I saw it demonstrated in the workplace. Over the years, I have measured the work volume of hundreds of white collar units. When the amount of work in a white collar unit is measured—in person-hours of work to be completed—and then compared with actual person-hours available to do the work, the hours of work to be completed generally represent between 45 and 55 percent of the hours available. At the low end of the scale, I have occasionally found units operating in the 30-percent range. Oddly enough, I have never come across a unit in the 60-percent range.

There are situations in which this is not clear-cut, such as when measuring office units with a backlog of work. But even in these cases, when the amount of work processed through a given unit is measured, I find the work is being handled at only about a 50-percent efficiency level.

For Example

Following are some examples of the 4/8 Theory taken from productivity improvement projects recently installed by Creative Management Alternatives.

11

Example 1:

A processing and technical unit of 151 employees (hours accumulated over 1 week).

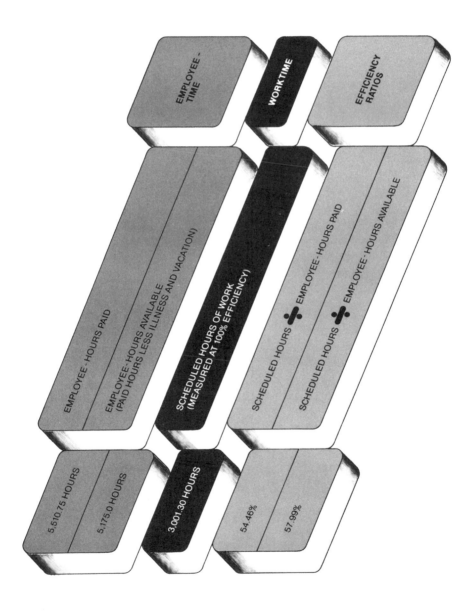

Example 2:

A processing and technical unit of 68 employees (hours accumulated over 1 week).

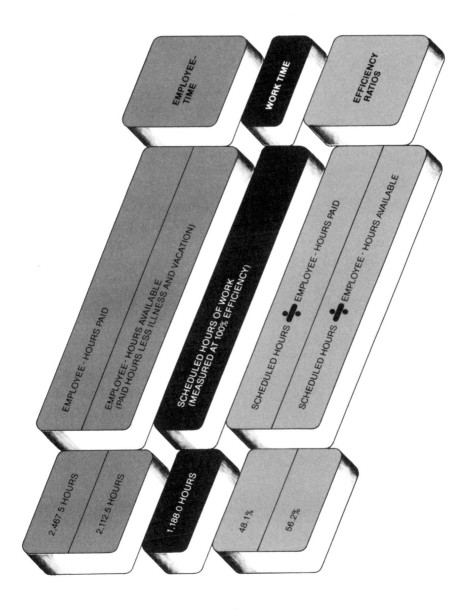

Example 3:

A processing and technical unit of 60 employees (hours accumulated over 1 week).

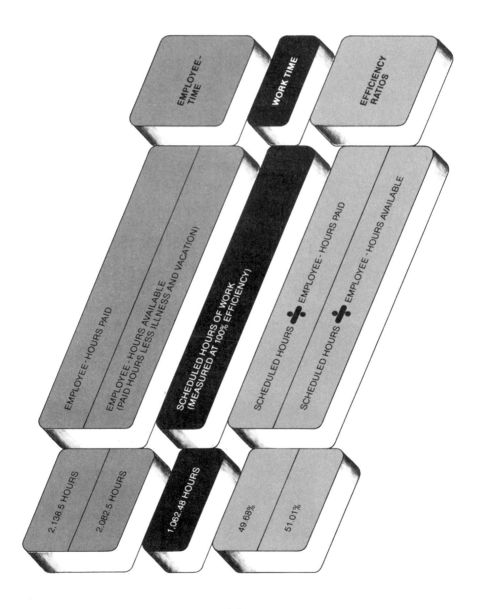

Example 4:

A processing and technical unit of 194 employees (hours accumulated over 9 days).

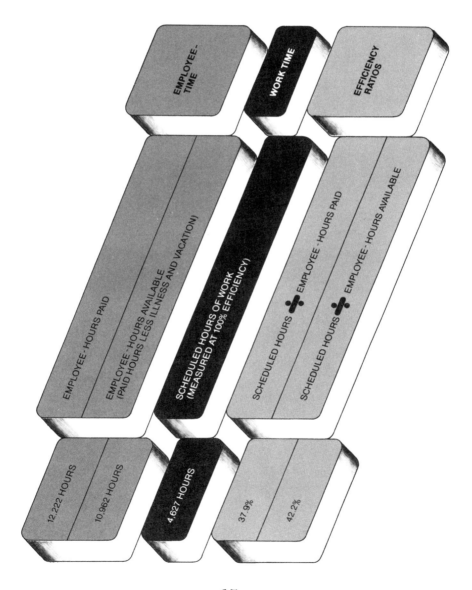

Example 5:

Total of preceding examples (473 employees).

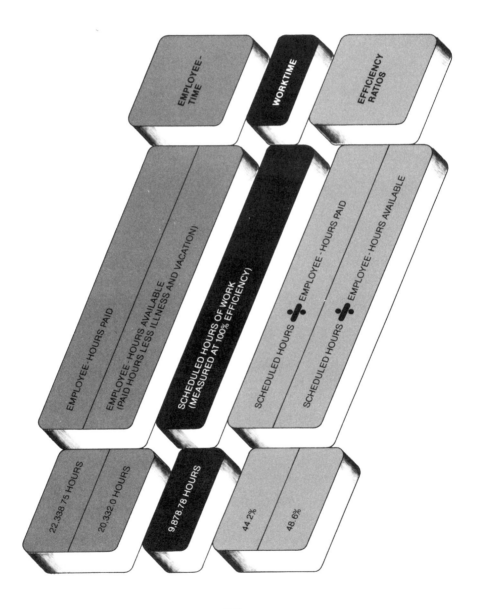

As you can see from these examples, the figure 4/8 is used in a general, or symbolic, sense rather than as a statement of fact. Also, very few office workers put in an eight-hour day. The average white collar employee, after coffee and lunch breaks, works a net of about 7.25 hours a day. But who would ever remember the 3.625/7.25 Theory? The 4/8 Theory is much easier to hold on to and, more important, it correlates closely with the disturbing reality that white collar employees today generally produce at only about a 50-percent efficiency level.

At the very outset, one must understand that the four hours of lost time are not four hours of recoverable time. Four hours of work for eight hours of pay constitutes an unsatisfactory productive effort. At the other extreme, expecting eight hours of continuous, uninterrupted effort is not only unrealistic but also immoral.

A Reasonable Work Expectation

If we cannot expect white collar workers to produce eight hours of continuous effort, what is a reasonable expectation? Or, put another way, how much of the four hours lost each day in a typical American office can we recover?

Because white collar productivity is a people issue, it is fair to say that there is no exact answer. We should all agree, however, that eight hours a day of continuous, uninterrupted effort is an efficiency level reserved for machines, not people. We now have the parameters of the issue established. The answer lies between 4/8 and 8/8. At this point, I can turn only to experience and professional logic as a guide. When a productivity improvement program is installed, there are a variety of results. The content of the program and the experience and knowledge level of the installers can be controlled. The third leg of the triad is the variable: the competency and cooperation of the unit in which the program is installed. When I have had maximum control over the three legs of the triad, productivity has improved by 40 to 50 percent. I feel this range

17

is the optimum. Therefore, our goal is 75-percent efficiency, or a 6/8 achievement. Stated in terms of our theory, we can reasonably expect to receive six hours of effective effort spread over eight hours of time available for work.

Here are two typical examples among many that have helped shape my opinion regarding 6/8 as a theoretical optimum achievement level. I chose them because not only did they start at the 4/8 level, but also the units involved cooperated to the utmost. Therefore I am confident that the results were the best that could be achieved.

Example 6:

In May 1976, we installed a productivity enhancement system in the processing and underwriting function of a medium-sized insurance company. Before we did so, the company had measured productivity as transactions per employee per month. The 12 months before our involvement had been a period of stable productivity. In that 12-month period, the company produced 4,237,994 transactions over 3,599.49 employee-months. Stated another way, a monthly average of 299.96 processing and underwriting employees performed 1,177.4 transactions on an individual monthly basis.

Then we installed our program. (See table 1.)

Table 1

Project Period (Measured in Quarters of Activity from Project Date of 5/1/76)	Average Employee Count Per Month	Transactions Per Employee	% Improvement Over Base
Base	299.9	1177.4	− 0 −
1st Quarter	286	1402	+19.1%
2nd Quarter	275	1470	+24.9%
3rd Quarter	248	1659	+40.9%
4th Quarter	251	1650	+40.1%
5th Quarter	265	1815	+54.2%
6th Quarter	284	1761	+49.6%

During this same period, the company dramatically increased the ratio of policies in force to processing employee. At the end of the fourth quarter, this ratio had climbed by 28.5 percent over base; and by the end of the sixth quarter, the ratio had climbed by 46.2 percent.

At the beginning of the productivity improvement project, the company was processing 1,407.2 policies in force per processing/underwriting employee. Eighteen months later, the insurance company easily passed 2,000 policies per employee. Today, it is using computer improvements to work its way to a 4,000-policy-per-employee goal. Before this project, the company was considered very efficient by industry standards. After installing the system, I concluded that it was as productive an operation as could reasonably be expected. Project results such as these lead to the conclusion that 6/8 represents the practical limits of white collar efficiency.

Example 7:

The next example concerns the installation of a productivity enhancement system in a commercial insurance processing division. Before installation, this division measured at a 50-percent efficiency level (4/8). We installed the system in January. By the end of December, the division's productivity improvement ratios read as shown in table 2.

Table 2

Audit Inside	+25.9%
Loss Control Inside	+67.3%
Underwriting	+36.0%
Customer Accounting	+26.9%
Policywriting	+68.8%
Rating & Coding	+48.1%
Machine Production	+29.1%
Records	+17.0%
TOTAL	+41.6%

Productivity improved so dramatically in this division in part because within 60 days after we installed the productivity improvement program, the division added three states to its territory. This increased the division's workload by 27.6 percent over the like period in the previous year. Almost from the beginning, a 9.8-percent smaller work force processed the additional work than had in the like period in 1980.

This example illustrates that my comments can be taken only as generalities, not as absolutes. The example shows clearly the varied scope of both the 4/8 Theory and the 6/8 Theory.

In insurance, one lives by the law of large numbers. If the law is large numbers, then part of the code is "the mix" and "the mill run." The 4/8 and the 6/8 are merely symbols to help get the point across: White collar waste is manageable. For white collar waste to be manageable, we must be able to define its limits, its presence, and its tangibleness. If we are to manipulate it, we have to get a handle on it. Example 7 also illustrates two other very important points about productivity improvement that relate to growth and management.

Productivity and Growth

First, it is far easier to improve employee productivity when markets are expanding than when they are frozen or shrinking. Unfortunately, we tend to think about productivity only when markets are shrinking, which means we must reduce staff in one way or another.

There is an inherent difficulty in maximizing productivity benefits in a down cycle. Management and employees respond aggressively and affirmatively to the challenge of growth. When you install your productivity improvement system in a growth cycle, you have the added luxury of riding the growth momentum. In a down cycle, management and employees respond defensively. It is quite possible that, all things being equal, a 30- to 40-percent productivity gain in a production up cycle would only be a 10- to 20-percent gain in a down cycle. You can improve productivity by the 30 to 40 percent in a down cycle, but you will tax the determination of the work unit's management.

20

The nation as a whole is talking productivity today because we have just experienced a severe down cycle. The United States will make gains, but we will make far greater gains if we continue the productivity discipline during the economic recovery and beyond. In truth, productivity improvement is a permanent discipline.

Productivity and Management

The second point example 7 makes is the dependence of any productivity improvement program and installation methodology on client management. In example 7, units improved from 17 percent to 68.8 percent. The example gives you the opportunity to look at each unit separately. In this case, we have built-in test controls. The company management, the installation team, the system, the location, and the timing were identical for all units. The only variables among units were the training, attitude, and experience of the individual employees and their supervisors. (We discuss the advisability of hiring outside consulting help in chapter 13. When we get to that chapter, remember example 7 when I say that no productivity improvement approach can rise above the managerial competency of the client.)

The insurance company and commercial lines insurance, examples 6 and 7, support a theory. A ratio of 4/8 is a substantially accurate representation of the huge amount of waste that the present American office system produces. The 6/8 ratio is also a realistic representation of the scope of improvement within reasonable reach through an effective system for upgrading productivity.

These are the theories as they have been formulated to this point:

The 4/8 Theory:

The average white collar work unit performs work at a 50-percent efficiency level.

As we are dealing with people, we cannot expect efficiency levels of 90 to 100 percent. These levels are reserved for machines.

The 6/8 Theory:

White collar work units are capable of achieving efficiency levels of 75 percent.

The Frontline Worker

To understand the 4/8 Theory, we must dispatch the notion that the white collar worker is responsible for the productivity problem. Granted, four hours of effective work for eight hours of pay rings out like an indictment of the entire white collar work force. But that is just not the case. I have yet to see a group of white collar workers who will not respond to reasonable work direction from management. Therein lies a clue.

For simplicity's sake, let's translate our 4/8 and 6/8 theories from hours into minutes. We can expect 45 minutes of productive effort out of every 60 minutes of paid time (6/8). We are now getting into a very sophisticated area of productivity management. I do not mean that we condone a 15-minute break each hour. What I mean, rather, is that 45 minutes of concentrated effort spread over 60 minutes elapsed time is a reasonable goal and certainly far more productive than the 30 minutes of concentrated effort spread over each hour that the average American office is getting today.

White collar waste is not a problem of individual employees. We must consider the individual employee, but more in terms of how that individual relates to the working group. When you feel an employee in your office can be more productive, you must first determine where that employee's productivity problem lies. We usually assume that individuals are not productive because they don't work hard enough. From this, many conclude that they are not working fast enough.

In reality, the average employee usually works at a speed commensurate with his or her training and experience. Workers do not deliberately work slowly. They either work or they don't work. In other words, the perceived ineffectualness of their performance is the result of the time they spend *not working*, not in *working slowly*. I characterize the worker's performance as "perceived ineffectualness" because it is popular to blame the employee for wasted office time. The individual employee is not to blame. Office time is wasted because management does not know how to manage it. The best example of the perception that the employee is to blame can be found in a question I am often asked: "In your 4/8 Theory, what are the employees doing during the lost 4 hours?" Who cares? The problem is not what *is* happening, but what is *not* happening. We are *not* managing. The individual employee is not the productivity issue.

This point was driven home a number of years ago during analysis of the results of a very successful productivity improvement program. Before the program, the unit—a typing unit—had been performing at 50-percent effectiveness. (Incidentally, I use typing units several times in this book as productivity examples, because many people view typing skill as a rate issue, e.g., 60 words per minute.)

In the case in point, the unit's typists were at a skill level of 50 to 70 words per minute. We installed a productivity improvement system that increased their productivity by close to 50 percent. The question then was, if the average output per typist was increased 50 percent, what had happened to the typists' speeds? We all know the answer. They had stayed the same. The 50-percent productivity gain did not come from increased speed; it resulted from the typists making more efficient use of their time.

Work Speed

Productivity improvement has nothing to do with causing people to work faster. This is a myth that has to be destroyed once and for all.

Granted, productivity is rooted in training and experience. Therefore, in training an employee, one of our goals is to work at getting the employee up to speed. At the company or corporate level, this is a training issue, not a productivity issue. Throughout this book, I assume that the necessary training and experience-gathering have been accomplished. Therefore, speed is not a white collar productivity issue. I also assume that we are not dealing with the underqualified or overqualified employee. We are not discussing individual characteristics or temporary efficiency-diminishing issues such as headaches or hangovers. Now we are putting our finger on the essence of white collar productivity as a manageable issue. To improve white collar productivity, we must find a way for the average employee to concentrate on performing a given job for 45 minutes an hour rather than 30 minutes. The white collar productivity improvement issue resolves itself to something as basic as expanding 30 minutes of concentrated effort to 45 minutes of concentrated effort spread over an hour.

This is quite different from blue collar productivity, which is machine-associated. In blue collar productivity, rate of activity is very important; in fact, it is the key issue. White collar productivity, on the other hand, is primarily associated with efficient use of time—the efficient use of the day. White collar productivity and blue collar productivity are different. We must be cautious when we apply blue collar thinking to white collar situations.

As noted, rate has a white collar significance when associated with the new, inexperienced worker. But, given the employee's training and experience, we must accept the employee on the merits of her or his ability. *When an employee is working within his or her ability limits and those limits are consistent with the job description, we have no right to press for more rate.*

If you don't carefully present these points to your employees, they will misinterpret your corporate productivity enhancement programs to mean they must speed up their work. You may already have work-measurement systems in operation. If you do not understand the 4/8 Theory, and if your employees do not understand the 4/8 Theory, why will your employees think you installed a work-measurement system? They can only assume that you want increased rate or, to put it in the employees' words, "to make us work harder and faster." It's a natural assumption.

Let's go a step further. Without the help of management to organize their time, how else can employees personally respond to work measurement but with what they consider the only answer, increased speed? Think about that a minute. If you press for increased productivity without helping employees plan and organize their work, *you* force your employees to see the issue as one of rate.

On the following statement, I stake my reputation: *Significant, durable, white collar efficiency improvement is founded in the managed, efficient use of the day.*

What Is the Issue?

If the 4/8 Theory accurately describes the problem, why are we presently getting only 30 minutes of effort out of each hour? Is it:

- Diminished work ethic?
- Boredom?
- The "me" generation?
- Unfulfilling work?
- Lack of challenge?
- Inadequate motivation?
- A management problem?

25

By now it must be obvious that I feel America's present low productivity is a management problem. The white collar productivity issue is confused today because many think of it as a social problem. Today's fast track to fame and fortune is to discuss productivity on a sociological plane and to contrast ourselves culturally with Japan.

It is popular to start texts on productivity by exposing the reader statistically to the belief that America has all the problems, Japan has all the answers. I agree that we have productivity and quality problems, but I also feel we have the answers. When we want to look the productivity dilemma in the eye, we can do so by looking in the mirror. Today, Japanese executives are giving us productivity jitters. A broad group of business executives across this country have had their thinking on productivity channelled to the mysterious, to the inscrutable. That is a problem in itself. Because the Japanese are our competitors in the marketplace, Japanese executives are probably quite pleased to see our anxiety.

Business constantly faces the Gordian knot of simultaneously maintaining growth and profit. A company lives or dies in the marketplace by the swords of quality, service, and price. The Japanese have a head start on unravelling the knot. They understand that you can have quality, service, and price without having to worry about outstanding productivity . . . but only for a while, because then you open the window of vulnerability to your competitors. That's the popular theory of what has happened in the United States. The compelling aspect of improving productivity is that it enhances quality and service and drives down price. That is Japan's secret. American top management today has been psyched into accepting the myth that the Japanese have all the answers while we have all the problems. The productivity issue is neither enigmatic nor inscrutable. Rather, it is susceptible to logical analysis and is approachable through common sense.

The cloak of mystery that surrounds the productivity issue is not just perceived as oriental; we have added to the mystery by simmering it in a bowl of alphabet theory soup. Many can discuss the theories of X, Y, and Z; and yet no one can solve the white collar productivity dilemma. Improving quality-of-work-life is necessary, and a cooperative attitude among government, management, and labor is desirable. Many, however, misunderstand the fact that quality-of-work-life programs must rely on a well-managed base. Quality-of-work-life programs are not a substitute for good management.

We like to discuss productivity in terms of the employee work ethic. A corporate need for a positive work ethic is a need to force employees to rely on their natural instincts as a crutch for the lack of good management. The problem does not lie in the unresponsiveness of employees, but rather it stems from management's failure to provide proper attention and direction in the first place. In other words, effective management can substantially improve productivity, even in cases in which employee attitudes are indifferent. *The ultimate productivity enhancement is the blossoming of quality-of-work-life techniques out of a sound management foundation.*

If I am wrong, there's no hope. The United States is not going to become a Japan. We cannot wait the generations it will take (if ever) to return to the positive work ethic that supposedly prevailed 50 years ago and do nothing about management.

If today's work ethic is a harbinger of the future, then we are better off accepting it and tightening up our management style. The American worker is not the problem. Our workers are suffering right along with corporate profit-and-loss statements as they wait for American management to assert itself and provide leadership. If you do not believe that statement, ask the opinion of the laid-off auto or steel worker. In the long run, good productivity does not lay off employees; bad productivity closes plants.

I have discussed 4/8 and 6/8. We have the potential to improve productivity by 50 percent. Within each and every employee there resides a potential additional half person, trained and ready to go to work. Our challenge is to identify that half person and properly use the resource.

3

White Collar Productivity:
The Reality

We have discussed the 4/8 Theory in detail. Now the question is: What is the nature of the issue we are dealing with; what is white collar productivity?

We now have the building blocks of knowledge needed to construct an answer to the obvious question the 4/8 Theory poses. Today, white collar productivity experts are running the wrong course in search of the "Productivity Grail." They generally assume that to increase white collar productivity, they must find methods to develop a capacity for greater output within the white collar ranks.

In view of the 4/8 Theory, we might instead ask, "What do we do with the excess capacity that presently exists?" We already have the capacity for greater output. The Productivity Grail is within our midst. *Our task is not to create capacity but to recover and manage the excess capacity we already have.*

As I have pointed out, this situation is pregnant with possibility. We have all read articles prophesying that new technology could lead to a U.S. staffing crisis in the nineties.

Tomorrow is today. Unfortunately, it was also yesterday, but we did not recognize it.

Work Capacity

Let's sharpen our focus. What is white collar work capacity? White collar work capacity is like vodka. You can't smell it, taste it, or see it, but it is nevertheless powerful.

The major problem with this subject is that we are used to managing tangibles. As an example, let's take a unit of 10 people. If all 10 employees show up for work and work an 8-hour day, you know that you will pay for 80 hours of work. But we never think in terms of how many hours of work they actually do or how many hours of work need to be done.

Let's use that 10-employee unit as an example. Say the 4/8 rule applies, and the unit is usually current. What this means is, not only does 50-percent efficiency prevail, but it is sufficient to do the job. Therefore, the unit's average daily workload is 40 hours of work, not the 80 hours you are paying for. (See figure 1.) Time passes, and this unit of 10 employees is now blessed with good productivity management that takes them to a 75-percent efficiency level (6/8). With the unit's efficiency increased by 50 percent, 10 actual employees now represent a full-time equivalent (FTE) of 15 employees in terms of the constant 40 hours of work to be performed. (See figure 2 on page 32.) Then, let's say all of the 10 employees (now 15 FTE employees) leave the unit permanently. They are replaced, and the unit now consists essentially of trainees. (It has been my experience that trainees start at a 30- to 35-percent efficiency level.) Since they are trainees, all 10 employees are functioning at a productivity level of 35 percent. What previously was a unit with the FTE of 15 employees (10 employees working at 75-percent efficiency) now has the FTE of 7 employees (10 employees working at 35-percent efficiency). (See figure 3 on page 33.)

PAID CAPACITY ACTUAL CAPACITY

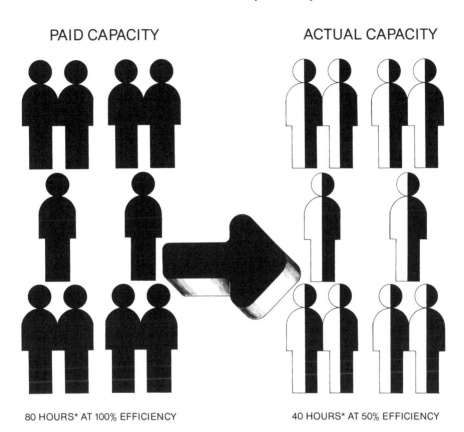

80 HOURS* AT 100% EFFICIENCY   40 HOURS* AT 50% EFFICIENCY

*AT 8 HOURS PER EMPLOYEE

Figure 1

If you had 10 employees and hire 5, only then to lose 8, you would clearly understand the implications of those circumstances on your unit's work output. It is much more difficult to grasp the effect on office production when a unit keeps a constant number of employees and goes through an efficiency cycle of 50 percent to 75 percent to 35 percent (which is the same as 10 to 15 to 7 FTE employees).

Variations on this phenomenon can be endless. For example, let's take the original 10 employees, but with the range of individual efficiencies as shown in example 1 on page 33.

31

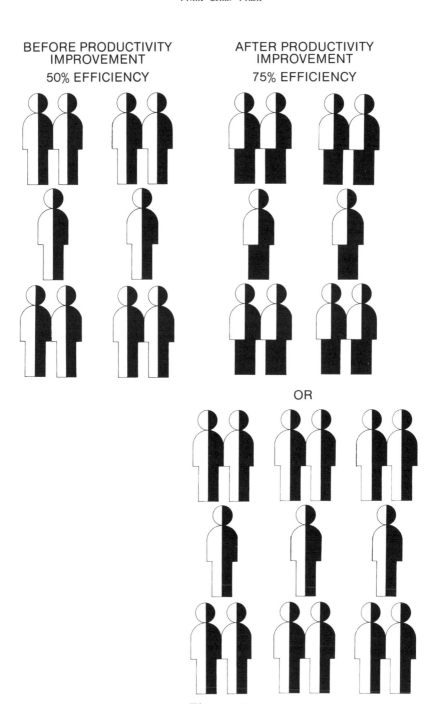

Figure 2

TRAINEES AT
35% EFFICIENCY

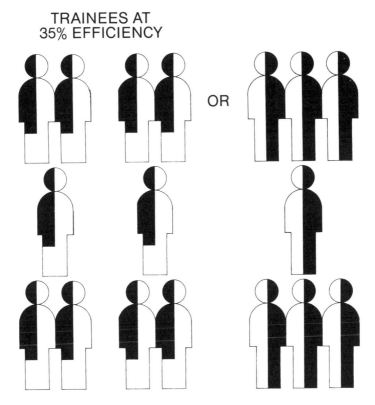

Figure 3

Example 1:

Two employee trainees at 30% efficiency
Two semitrained employees at 40% efficiency
Four average employees at 50% efficiency (4/8 average)
Two superior employees at 80% efficiency

TOTAL UNIT EFFICIENCY: 50%

The two trainees are equivalent to 1.2 average employees
The two semitrained are equivalent to 1.6 average employees
The four average employees are equivalent to 4.0 employees
The two superior employees are equivalent to 3.2 average
   employees

TOTAL: 10 actual employees equal 10 equivalent employees

33

When the productivity of the trainees and the semitrained employees improves to the point that it matches the average level of 50 percent, you then have an equivalent work force of 11.2 employees. Our original hypothesis was that the unit's workload required 40 hours of work. We now have 44.8 hours of potential people-effort available. That means that the unit supervisor could easily reduce the staff by one person. You and I know that will not happen because: 1) the supervisor will not see what is happening, and 2) we do not give our supervisors motivation to increase productivity.

Let's return to example 1. We now have 44.8 employee-effort hours available to perform 40 hours of work with no staff reduction. What has happened to our productivity? It is forced to remain at 50 percent. "Hey! Wait a minute. You just said that the efficiency of the trainees and the semitrained went up to 50 percent; that means that the whole unit's efficiency went to 56 percent, or it now has 11.2 equivalent employees." That's correct, in terms of *potential* efficiency. But because the workload did not increase and/or the labor hours were not reduced, the efficiency level was forced to conform to the 40 hours of work available.

What have I just said?

First, we probably lost some of the efficiency gained by bringing the undertrained employees up to the average efficiency. We also lowered the efficiency of the remaining members of the unit, because there was only so much work to do. I have said that white collar productivity is a management problem, not an employee issue. Yet, I continue to talk in terms of employees taking eight hours of pay for four hours of effort. I know that statement may not please some of you—no matter how much I protest that the issue is a management one, not an employee one. As example 1 demonstrates, however, we have 10 employees with unacceptable productivity levels forced on them by poor management.

If you have 10 employees handling 40 hours of work and their efficiency level improves through training and/or experience and you neither increase the work they have to do nor decrease the staff, *you* have trapped the employees.

What goes through an employee's mind in this situation? The employee already knows how hard he or she is working. Do you really expect the employees to have any respect for supervisors, managers, or the company from that set of facts? If you want intraoffice bickering, boredom, low respect for the company and management, an overflowing rumor mill, and bad morale, just underutilize your employees.

How Underutilized Employees Adapt

Employees do not stretch work and force management to adapt. It's just the other way around: weak management allows the pace of the workflow to slow down, often in imperceptible stages. Then what happens? After a while, the new pace becomes normal. It also becomes inelastic. It does not spontaneously contract to assimilate additional work. I do not understand why this happens. It just seems to be a rule of human nature, one of Parkinson's laws.

In example 1, we had two superior employees working at 80-percent efficiency. Assuming they are promoted, let's see what happens. In example 1, we had two employees who worked at 30-percent efficiency, two who worked at 40-percent efficiency, four who worked at 50-percent efficiency, and the two who worked at 80-percent efficiency, making up a 50-percent efficiency average. First, we must understand that the problem is not simply limited to the two 80-percent-efficiency employees leaving. It also includes their replacement by two trainees who work at 30-percent efficiency. Now the office productivity level drops from 50 percent to 40 percent, which means a 20-percent loss in productivity. As a result, the unit has only 32 hours of effort to perform 40 hours of work.

How does the supervisor solve this dilemma? The supervisor understands the issue of trained and untrained workers. But what the supervisor does not clearly comprehend is, even though the unit still has the same number of employees, the work potential of the unit's staff has been reduced 20 percent.

35

Two employees left, and both were replaced. Yet, the unit is actually suffering a net loss of two equivalent workers.

In most cases the response to this situation is totally predictable. The supervisor calls for overtime and solves the problem at the expense of the individual employee. When first line management manages in an inept fashion, it covers itself at the expense of the employee. First line management's only crutch is the employee. The downside risk is that the supervisor will convince management to add one or possibly two new employees.

Earlier I noted that the variations on this efficiency theme can be endless. Here are three more:

1. Sickness and/or vacation. One day both trainees are gone (2 out of 10). The next day both superior employees are gone (2 out of 10). Was staff capacity down 20 percent on each of these days? No, it suffered a 20-percent loss on neither day. The first day the staff was down 1.4 equivalent employees (14 percent), while the next day the staff was down 3.2 equivalent employees (32 percent).

2. Suppose your two superior employees attended a party the night before and now come to work a little hung over (not well-motivated for that day), and their efficiency drops by half. In terms of efficiency, your equivalent work staff is down 1.6 employees, even though all 10 employees show up.

3. What about spring fever? Everyone comes in at 8 a.m. in a mood of normal work motivation, but by 11 a.m. spring fever hits the whole staff. How many equivalent employees do you have working that afternoon? Certainly not a full able crew.

The History of Management as the Problem

Before we leave this subject, let me describe how management, not the employee, could be responsible for the decline to the point where we get only four hours of productive work for eight hours of pay.

Scene I, 1940. The scenario begins with a unit of 10 employees right out of the olden days. These 10 employees are dripping with work ethic. Each employee is 80-percent efficient, because that is the American way. If these 10 employees work 8 hours a day and can adequately handle the unit's work, then we can assume that the unit has 64 hours of work to perform. This 64 hours of work divided by 80 available hours equals 80-percent efficiency.

10 employees, 80-percent efficient, 64 hours of work

We have a match: 64 productive hours and 64 hours of work.

Scene II, 1950. Two of our employees retire and are replaced by two trainees. Each trainee produces at an effective level of 30 percent.

8 employees, 80-percent efficient,	51.2	productive hours
2 employees, 30-percent efficient,	4.8	productive hours
TOTAL	56.0	productive hours

Now, we no longer have a match. Still needing 64 productive hours, the office is in trouble. The productivity of the two new employees is increasing, but not fast enough. So, an additional employee is hired. Time resolves the problem; eventually, all 11 employees are equally efficient. Remember, though, there are still only 64 hours of work to perform. Therefore:

11 employees, 72.7-percent efficient, 64 hours of work

Scene III, 1960. After 10 years, 72.7-percent efficiency has become standard. The 64 hours of work available have been stretched to accommodate the 11 employees.

Three of the employees leave for greener employment pastures, each of whom is replaced by a trainee who works at 30-percent efficiency.

8 employees, 72.7-percent efficient,	46.5	productive hours
3 employees, 30-percent efficient,	7.2	productive hours
TOTAL	53.7	productive hours

By this time the office has reached the crisis stage: it is short 16 percent of its production capacity, even though there are 11 employees. What does management do?

You guessed it; it upgrades the trainees but also adds the twelfth employee to perform the 64 hours of work that have remained constant. Therefore:

12 employees, 66.7-percent efficient, 64 hours of work

Scene IV, 1970. After 10 years, 66.7-percent efficiency becomes the standard. Now the five original employees, all in their declining years, retire. Crisis time again. We replace all five employees with trainees.

7 employees, 66.7-percent efficient, 37.4 productive hours
5 employees,   30-percent efficient, <u>12.0</u> productive hours
TOTAL <u>49.4</u> productive hours

This is the worst situation yet. The five retirees have been replaced, but the office is still short 22.8-percent productive hours. With the unit's backlog building at over 100 percent per week, three additional people are brought aboard out of desperation.

Scene V, 1980. What is our productivity situation?

15 employees, 53.3-percent efficient, 64 hours of work

The unit now probably gets by with an occasional employee leaving, because the trainee will come in at 30 percent and only have to improve to 53.3 percent to meet the new, reduced average. While the trainee is making this progress, the remaining 14 employees individually have no problem at all picking up the extra 8 minutes per day of work that the developing trainee burdens them with. Yes, the math is correct. This last point illustrates why falling efficiency levels hit a point of diminishing marginal return (negative) in the 45- to 55-percent range.

This simplistic scenario has brought us to 4/8 efficiency through no fault of the employees. It has occurred solely because management either ignored or was not aware that productivity is an issue. The next chapter in this book is on measurement. Keep the above scenario in mind as you read the section on macromeasurement. The events described in this chapter could not have occurred had macromeasurement been in effect.

The time frame of the scenario is also interesting. As I said earlier, I have been aware of the 4/8 Theory for 20 years. I am personally out of sync with the social revolution that hit this country in the late sixties and the seventies. It would give me great pleasure to be able to document that that social revolution was a major contributor to our white collar productivity problem. *My experience shows, however, that the problem of wasted white collar capacity was just as bad before the social revolution of the sixties and that it has not worsened because of it.*

The History of the 4/8 Theory

I am now going to wade into some very murky philosophical waters. If I am correct in saying that the 4/8 Theory existed 20 years ago, why not 50 years ago? Now for the murky waters. I have always felt that there was an unanswered question in the Hawthorne experiments. As you may recall, one of these famous experiments was designed to test the effect of lighting on employee output at Western Electric. The group that received better lighting increased their output. In addition, the control group that did not receive better lighting also increased their output. And to the consternation of management, output continued to increase in the experimental group when lighting was decreased.

As a result of this and many additional experiments, the conclusion was drawn that logical factors were not as important as emotional factors in enhancing worker output. Simplistically stated, these workers were responding positively to attention, to involvement, to participation. It is also interesting that not only did workers increase their output, but also they demonstrated less fatigue. The psychological implications were enormous.

But . . .

where did those employees at Western Electric find the additional capacity to increase their output? There is no indication that they were inspired to work harder and faster, to race through their chores. In fact, the experience was less fatiguing. The individuals in question did not sprout additional hands and arms. They did not increase their work experience with the flip of a light switch. Then where did the extra work capacity come from? Could it be that, before the experiment, Western Electric employees had been performing four hours of work for eight hours of pay? If so, then perhaps an enthusiastic response to attention coupled with a large, unmanaged work capacity gave us the "Hawthorne Effect."

The Intangibility of Unmanaged White Collar Work Capacity

The following examples further demonstrate the intangibility of white collar work capacity.

Example 2:

Say you have 100 people working for you. Output is well matched to input. Therefore, productivity is not an issue. You come to work Monday morning and find that three employees have placed resignations on your desk. That is a very tangible experience. Three people are leaving. Since productivity is not an issue, they had better be replaced.

Now let's change the scenario and say that the same 100 employees are distracted by a variety of things that happen in their office. The result of these "things" is that the attention of each one of these employees is diverted from her or his work effort to the extent of 1.8 seconds—two snaps of a finger—each minute, or 9 seconds spread over 5 minutes.

Nine seconds every 5 minutes is 1.8 minutes spread over an hour.

The 1.8 minutes per hour is 13 minutes spread over 7.25 work-hours in the average white collar day.

When you roll 13 minutes of lost time per day per employee into 100 employees' days, you have lost the equivalent of three employees. As the manager of a 100-employee unit, you are accustomed to authorizing the replacement of three people. You are not accustomed to replacing 13 minutes. Therefore, the plot thickens. Not only can you not recognize the loss of 13 minutes, but also, even if you could, you would be helpless to repair the situation. At $20,000 per employee, the utility of 60,000 payroll dollars has just slipped through your fingers.

Example 3:

Let's take 1 employee in a 100-employee unit. Let's say that employee quits. You are the boss. What will the supervisor responsible for that employee do? We all know the answer. That supervisor will submit an employee requisition.

Now for the rub.

What will *you* do?

Well, we know that answer too. You will consider replacing the employee. You will look at the requisition as an employee issue.

But is that the issue?

Based on the 4/8 Theory, what burden would you place on the remaining 99 employees (considering cross-training) if you did not replace that employee? Each of the 99 employees would have to absorb 2.4 minutes of additional work, or about 20 seconds of extra effort each hour.

Now, is the issue an employee issue or is it something as intangible as 20 seconds of effort per hour per 99 employees? Granted, in either case you might come to the same conclusion, but you have to admit your thought process would now be different. These are further examples of the intangibility of white collar waste. If you understand that fact, you are well on your way to solving your white collar productivity problem.

41

4

Measurement and Budgeting

To discuss white collar productivity, you must discuss measurement. Measurement is the rock upon which any white collar productivity improvement system must be built. This is an axiom. There are no exceptions. People commonly overlook this axiom when installing a blue collar productivity improvement system in a white collar operation.

Manufacturing has employed the so-called scientific method of management since the 1880's, when Fredrick Taylor found that the productivity of a worker using a hand shovel could be enhanced by designing the shovel to match the substance to be shoveled.

In manufacturing, industrial engineers are common.

In manufacturing, calibrated machines are the rule.

Manufacturers have employed scientific management for decades. They know that a given machine produces 100 widgets per hour, or 800 widgets per shift. A well-run manufacturing operation should know its present productivity level based on its present equipment. If a manufacturing plant knows where it is, then it can chart an intelligent course to where it wants to be. Note, I'm not saying that, because of measurement, the manufacturing industry is productive. I'm saying that the manufacturing industry should understand its productivity position.

This is not the case in the white collar arena. No salespeople come to us saying, "This is a 20-page-per-hour typewriter." Since measurement in white collar industries is not the general case, what are we admitting? We are admitting that most white collar operations do not know how productive they are from one day to the next. Further, if you do not know where you are, how do you know where you are going or how to get there? What productivity improvement tools do you use?

To use today's popular scale, you need to know where you stand on the productivity ladder of 1 to 10. If you are a two or a three, you don't need quality circles; you need an intensive care unit. If you are an eight, quality circles just might be the ticket.

The crucial question is, do you know where you are? I like to slot measurement into two general categories. I dislike using the terms, but "macro" and "micro" are popularly descriptive. In this chapter I won't discuss measurement techniques in depth but rather provide an opening overview of the subject. I want simply to introduce you to the subject of measurement and provide you with enough information to understand measurement and its importance.

Macromeasurement is the productivity measurement system that gauges the efficiency of your company, division, and unit.

Micromeasurement is the timing methodology used to measure individual tasks performed by your white collar employees.

Macromeasurement and Micromeasurement Are Often Confused

Today, there is no terminology popularly used to distinguish between the two types of measurement. You must distinguish between the two, however, because a neophyte to productivity improvement systems doesn't always understand

44

that there are two general categories of measurement and that they are used for different purposes.

I have often been asked, "What type of measurement system do you advocate?" The ensuing conversation can be confusing if I answer the question at the macro level when the question was asked at the micro level. This is particularly true when the questioner does not realize that there is a distinction. For example, the most recent such incident occurred while I was answering questions at a session of the Conference Board. Someone from the floor asked a measurement question. I answered the question at the macro level without qualifying my answer. Later in the conference, I found that I had confused several individuals who interpreted measurement as essentially a micro issue. They weren't even aware that macromeasurement existed as a discipline.

MACROMEASUREMENT

The basic productivity formula is

$$P = \frac{O}{I},$$

productivity equals output divided by input. Productivity measurement is a relationship of units, one to another. Productivity is not expressed exclusively as output or input. That may sound like a rather simplistic statement, but how many times have you inquired about the current state of your company's productivity by asking, "How many people have we dropped from our payroll?" (input). Or, "Why isn't the backlog down?" (output). Neither question addressed productivity. The first question was a staffing inquiry, and the second question was directed at production.

To enhance the overall perception of macromeasurement, let's ask these questions, "What is productivity, in a measurement sense?" and, "What does it mean?"

Simply stated, as I have said, productivity is output over input and, by itself, this definition has limited meaning. If you produce 800 widgets per shift (output) through the efforts of 10 employees (input), your resulting productivity ratio is 80 widgets per employee per shift. Only in this limited sense have you identified productivity.

Who cares?

Is 80 widgets per employee per shift good, bad, or indifferent? Who knows?

The Meaning of Measurement

If there was ever a subject that depended upon relativity for its expression, it is productivity. It is like the person who grows up in a small community and thinks the tall buildings in it are enormous. It is not until that person first visits a large city and sees towering skyscrapers that he or she realizes the buildings back home are, in fact, tiny. Measurement will initially provide you with a productivity benchmark. However, it will not tell you where you rank on the scale of 1 to 10. At first, you will not know if your buildings are towering or tiny.

Logic tells you to consider your buildings undersized. Consequently, you will take an appropriate historical year, measure it, and say that's what your company looks like. The productivity level for that year becomes your benchmark. If you're prudent, you consider that this measurement indicates that your buildings are inadequate and then you immediately start a building project!

Enter the productivity change-ratio. At this writing, the United States remains the most productive country in the world. When the leading industrialized nations of the free world are listed in order of productivity, the United States is on top. Japan is currently on the bottom. Well, that being the case, why is everyone so worried about the productivity performance of the United States and so enthralled with that of the Japanese? The driving issue is the productivity change-ratio. The productivity change-ratio measures productivity progress or the lack thereof. When you list the leading industrial nations of the free world in productivity change-ratio order, Japan and the United States flip-flop. Japan goes to the top, and the United States goes to the bottom.

If current trends continue, Germany and France will pass the United States in productivity in the mid-eighties, and Japan will pass the United States in the next decade. If the United States is presently the most productive nation in the world, does that mean that we are currently highly productive, productive, or somewhat productive? No one knows. All we know is our position relative to other countries. We are completely in a fog when it comes to productivity assessment in an absolute sense. Progress is the issue.

Now 80 widgets per day per employee becomes meaningful, because it is a starting place from which you can measure progress. Measurement initially gives you a benchmark and then monitors your improvement. Quite commonly, your base year (period) will be your current year or last year. A large corporation is so active that even recent history soon turns into apples as compared to today's oranges.

Measurement and Competition

To summarize these points, if you do not have a measuring system in effect today, you do not know where you are or where you are going. And, if your competitors have a system, then you are in trouble.

I'm going to digress to give you a brief description of the trouble you might be in without knowing it. A productivity gain in labor output can be considered substantially as a direct offset to compensation. I use the phrase "direct offset" because it is illustrative. Let's take two direct competitors in the same industry. One is an American firm whose labor productivity

47

growth rate is the same as the U.S. 1979 projected productivity negative growth rate of –.9 percent.[2] The competing company is a Japanese firm whose labor productivity growth rate is the same as Japan's 1979 projected positive productivity growth rate of +4.5 percent.[3]

Each company gives its employees a 10-percent aggregate raise in compensation. The labor expenses of the American company will increase 10.9 percent. The additional compensation increases labor cost by 10 percent, while the productivity decline increases it .9 percent. At the same time, the Japanese company reduces labor expenses 4.5 percent, due to productivity increases. Adding a 10-percent increase in labor expenses results in a total increase in expenses of only 5.5 percent.

Here we have two competitors both using the same salary administration, only to have one company end the year with a 5.4 percent labor cost advantage.

I chose an international example so that I could use the juxtaposition of projected productivity growth rates of universal interest. The example is the same when you compare your company with a competitor. I'll say it again. If you do not know where you are on the productivity scale, you are lost. And if you do not know where you are but your competitors know where they are, you are in serious trouble.

Productivity measurement is a management blueprint.

In the preface, I characterized expenses as multidimensional. For example, currently white collar employees have an efficiency improvement range of 50 percent. This is within reach through sound management. Quality-of-work-life approaches will improve this projection. As an example, 80- to 85-percent efficiency is possible only through a highly motivated employee. But, the range of improvement does not end there. What about machine enhancements? How does a manager recognize and manipulate all these enhancements if they are not identified through measurement? Have you ever wondered why your managers do not manage their units, but just tend them?

---

[2] Projected Productivity Trends, GDP per Employee. (1978 U.S. = 100)
[3] *Ibid.*

48

Maybe the company is not providing the tools of real management.

I have discussed measurement in a simplistic fashion. In reality, productivity measurement is dynamic, thought-provoking, and a challenge to corporate management.

The Analysis of a Productivity Measurement Model

Today, the conventional way to analyze corporate progress is through financial reports—through the income statement. We operate, budget, and plan through the instruments of financial analysis. We measure our revenue. We measure our expenses. The difference between the two is our profit or loss. Expressed as a ratio, revenue over expense yields profitability.

We might display these issues as shown in figure 1 on page 50.

What is revenue?

Revenue is product price multiplied by quantity sold. This is very basic. It indicates that revenue is a function of price and quantity. Revenue can be displayed as shown in figure 2 on page 51.

The next question is, what are expenses?

Again it is quantity times cost; i.e., tons of steel times cost per ton; square feet of building space times cost per square foot; hours of labor times average wage per hour. It could be any one of those examples or all of them. For our purposes, let's take cost of labor, which could be displayed as shown in figure 3 on page 51.

Let's return to our time-honored financial analysis display of profits and losses as a function of the interaction between revenue and expenses. Now, however, we will enrich it by adding the basic components of revenue and expenses. We can display this as shown in figure 4 on page 52.

Figure 1

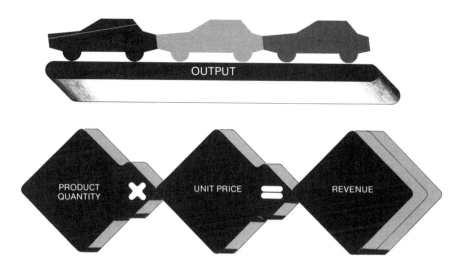

Figure 2

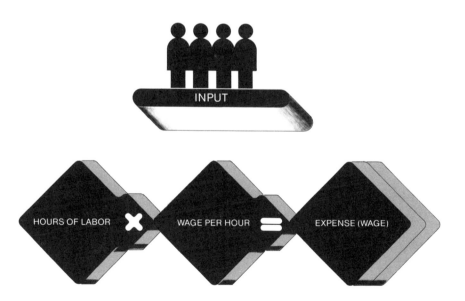

Figure 3

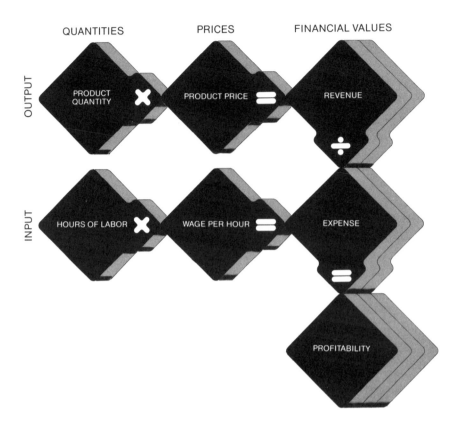

Figure 4

All right, I want to ask you a question. Do you see a relationship developing here that lends itself to more than just profit-and-loss analysis? That's right, productivity is the result of output (quantity sold) over input (hours of labor to produce the quantity). See figure 5.

QUANTITIES

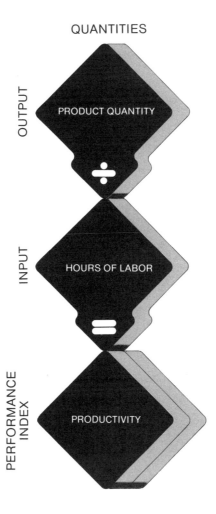

Figure 5

In a specific case, this might work out to:

$$\frac{1000 \text{ (quantity sold)}}{100 \text{ (hours of labor)}} = \text{Productivity index of 10 units per hour}$$

From figure 4, we can also determine the relationship between unit price and unit cost. See figure 6 on page 54.

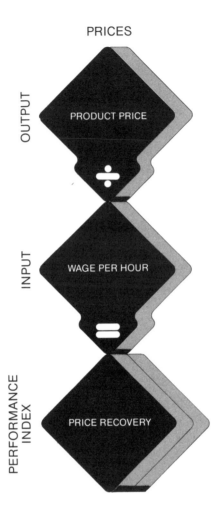

Figure 6

In a specific case, this might work out to:

$$\frac{\$100 \text{ (price per unit)}}{\$10 \text{ (average wage per hour)}} = \begin{array}{l} \text{Price recovery index of} \\ \$10 \text{ of unit price per} \\ \$1 \text{ of average wage} \end{array}$$

Figure 4 has now evolved to appear as shown in figure 7, or as shown in figure 8 on page 56.

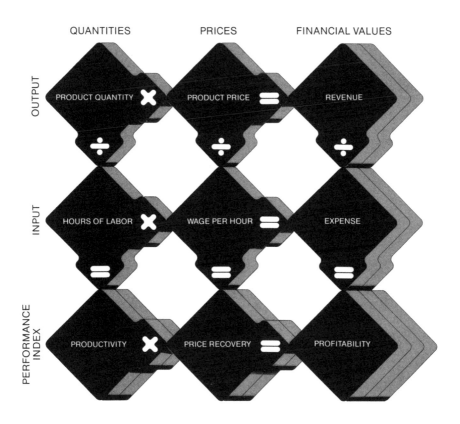

Figure 7

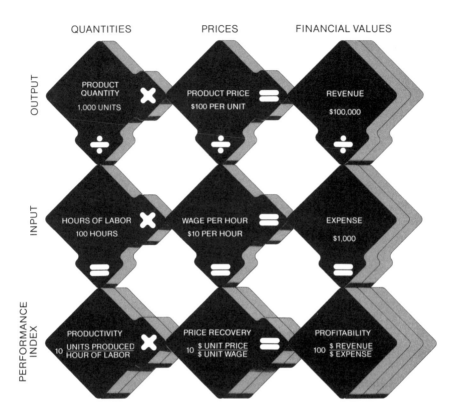

Figure 8

What does this tell us? Figure 8 has only limited value, because we do not know if the portrayal is good or bad. Is productivity of 10 units per employee-hour good? I don't know. Is price recovery of $10 of unit price per $1 hourly wage good? I don't know.

Let's take figure 8 and say it is the historical base period. Figure 9 positions the base period numbers (last year) against the current numbers (this year).

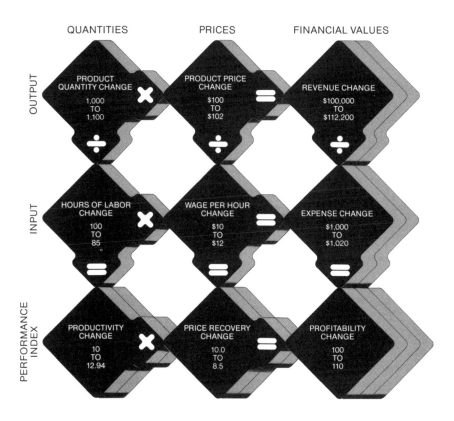

Figure 9

Now we come to the fundamental expression and substance of the macromeasurement model. We record change by
dividing the current period by the base period. The results are
change-ratios that, for ease of interpretation, I will convert to
plus or minus percent of change. Figure 10 on page 58 displays
the change-ratios that are a result of figure 9.

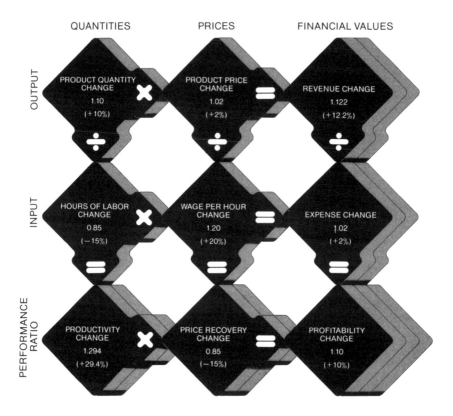

Figure 10

In figure 11, we have limited figure 10 to a financial analysis portrayal.

Since financial analysis is the popular method of analyzing corporate well-being, figure 11 tells us that the growth in revenue completely satisfies our increase in labor expense. Not only that, but it seems to show that revenue gave us a 10-percent increase in profitability.

FINANCIAL
VALUES

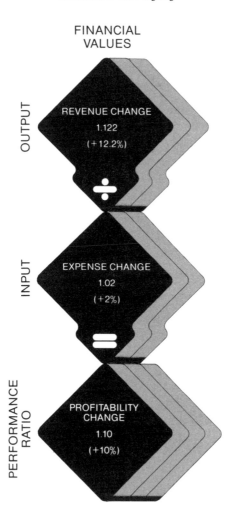

Figure 11

This analysis could not be further from the truth. Our labor unit cost change as it relates to our price change is the problem, with a shortfall in price recovery of 15.0 percent. The champion of the day is the 29.4-percent increase in productivity. See figure 12 on page 60.

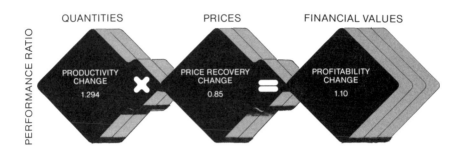

Figure 12

The questions then become rather obvious. How could we come to this conclusion without measuring productivity? Do we need this information? The answers are too obvious to recite.

Say figure 10 is a portrayal of your competition. Let's say the competition worries about productivity and employs productivity measurement. Further, let's say that you do not. You both draw from the same labor pool, so your salaries track with theirs. You both sell to the same customer pool, so your pricing activity cannot get out of line with theirs. Therefore, if you do not reap substantially the same productivity gains or you do not measure productivity, your competitor has you on the ropes. Worse yet, you won't know your competitor has you on the ropes for 12, 24, or some indeterminable number of months in the future.

In these examples I did not use total factor productivity on the input side of the equation. It is obvious that an expense shortfall in labor could be made up in economies in material, capital, and/or energy. I provide these examples not to make you an expert on productivity measurement but simply to make you aware of measurement—to whet your appetite.

Communicating Productivity Results through Measurement Reports

What is the full potential of measurement? How can we efficiently communicate measurement information?

Communication style is important. Pity the poor soul who feels the need to introduce another report into the corporate bureaucracy. Your productivity measurement information must be necessary, interesting, understandable, and attractively displayed. Example 1 contains four displays (tables 1—4), all based on the same productivity statistics, showing how to display labor productivity information effectively.

These displays will be called upon to do double-duty. In the first chapters of this text, I emphasized the 4/8 and 6/8 Theories not as absolutes but rather as descriptive, relative statements. I said that a 50-percent increase in efficiency was an achievable goal. Whether a specific unit attains it, however, depends heavily on the training and experience of the personnel in the unit as well as on the adequacy of the productivity improvement system and the capabilities of the installers.

Example 1:

This example contains the elements of a clinical laboratory experiment. Displayed are a variety of results that occurred as a result of:

1. the same productivity improvement system,

2. the same time frame,

3. the same installers,

4. the same client management group, and

5. the same location.

See table 1 on page 62.

The display in table 1 depicts the productivity labor-change-ratio factors of eight indicated expense units for the year ending December 31, 1981, as compared with the base year 1980. This particular office has about 100 employees, and each unit has 12 to 15 employees. The exception is the machine production unit, whose employee count was reduced to the

Table 1

PRODUCTIVITY MEASURES—BY OFFICE DIVISION X COMMERCIAL LINES			
PERIODS MEASURED BASE: 12 months ending December 31, 1980 CURRENT: 12 months ending December 31, 1981			
PRODUCTIVITY AND PRICING CHANGE			
Expense Units	Change in Productivity	Change in Price Recovery	Total Change in Profitability
Audit Inside	1.220	.820	1.000
Loss Control Inside	1.368	.870	1.190
Underwriting	1.237	.879	1.087
Customer Accounting	1.194	.854	1.020
Policywriting	1.577	.847	1.337
Rating and Coding	1.369	.848	1.160
Machine Production	.635	1.087	.691
Records	1.213	.926	1.124
TOTAL	1.291	.866	1.118

point where its figures are highly volatile. Since this is an insurance company display, the productivity output is measured by policies in force.

Let's evaluate the total by displaying it through the measurement model. See figure 13.

How would you like to be a competitor of Division X? Assume that in 1980 both of you started on an equal footing. Division X has a productivity improvement system and a method of productivity measurement. Your company has neither.

Division X improves its marketing position through price moderation. Your company can't afford to lose market share, so you follow suit by similarly lowering your prices.

Division X secures its technical expertise with an aggressive salary policy. Your company begins to sense an employee raid developing, and you follow suit.

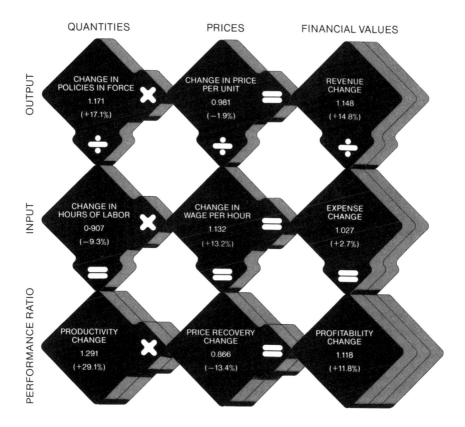

Figure 13

Unfortunately, you do not have a productivity measuring system, so you can't quantify what has happened. You do know that you have reduced your prices and increased your salaries. You do not know that your competitor has paid for this maneuver with increased productivity. You complain to your people because, "Expenses are out of hand." Without productivity measurement, you do not know how to assess the problem and take aggressive, corrective action.

I'll get off the soapbox now and return to the issue of displaying measurement results. The first display, in table 1, is a common productivity measurement display. This display is frequently used, because it reports the period in the form that emerges from the calculator.

When I discussed the results recorded in this display, I converted the factors to percentages. Why? Because that is the common way to interpret factors. Show a factor of .866 and what do you do? You mentally convert it to a percentage. Therefore, why not display the measurement output as a percentage? The next display (table 2) contains the same information as the first display (table 1, page 62).

Table 2

PRODUCTIVITY MEASURES—BY OFFICE DIVISION X COMMERCIAL LINES			
PERIODS MEASURED BASE: 12 months ending December 31, 1980 CURRENT: 12 months ending December 31, 1981			
PRODUCTIVITY AND PRICING CHANGE			
Expense Units	Change in Productivity	Change in Price Recovery	Total Change in Profitability
Audit Inside	22.0%	−18.0%	0.0%
Loss Control Inside	36.8	−13.0	19.0
Underwriting	23.7	−12.1	8.7
Customer Accounting	19.4	−14.6	2.0
Policywriting	57.7	−15.3	33.7
Rating and Coding	36.9	−15.2	16.0
Machine Production	−36.5	8.7	−30.9
Records	21.3	−7.4	12.4
TOTAL	29.1%	−13.4%	11.8%

Displaying a factor as a percentage provides not only the tool to make a statement of "good" or "bad" but also "how good or how bad." But it does not carry a tangible message. The next display (see table 3) does just that; it turns the simple statement of good or bad into the very tangible expression of dollar impact on profits. Table 3 contains the same information as tables 1 and 2.

Measurement and Budgeting

Table 3

PRODUCTIVITY MEASURES—BY OFFICE DIVISION X COMMERCIAL LINES			
PERIODS MEASURED BASE: 12 months ending December 31, 1980 CURRENT: 12 months ending December 31, 1981			
IMPACT ON PROFITS			
Expense Units	Productivity Impact	Price Recovery Impact	Total Impact On Profits
Audit Inside	$ 16,801	$ -16,794	$ 7
Loss Control Inside	20,226	-9,002	11,224
Underwriting	108,687	-64,726	43,961
Customer Accounting	29,012	-18,440	10,572
Policywriting	65,270	-24,749	40,521
Rating and Coding	85,003	-44,735	40,268
Machine Production	-2,694	359	-2,335
Records	14,374	-5,495	8,879
TOTAL	$336,679	$-183,582	$153,097

Note how much more interesting it is to see that the increased unit productivity of 29.1 percent represents an impact of $336,679 on profits. Finally, we have information displayed as a computer graph. See table 4 on page 66.

The graph in table 4 contains the same information as tables 1, 2, and 3. Its main advantage is in the display of a visual spatial relationship. You can use it to get a quick feel for the achievement relationship of the various units. A combination of the displays shown in tables 1—4 represents the most workable measurement reporting tool.

Obviously, the number of methods to display productivity measurement is far greater than shown in tables 1—4. I offer these four only to stimulate your appetite.

The improper display of measurement results is a common pitfall. Too often we do not balance the statistics to be reported against the interests of the audience. We feel that the audience needs the statistics. Therefore, we leave the statistics in a form that is dull and hard to analyze.

Two other measurement problems that arise are how to weight the data and how to decide what to measure.

65

Table 4

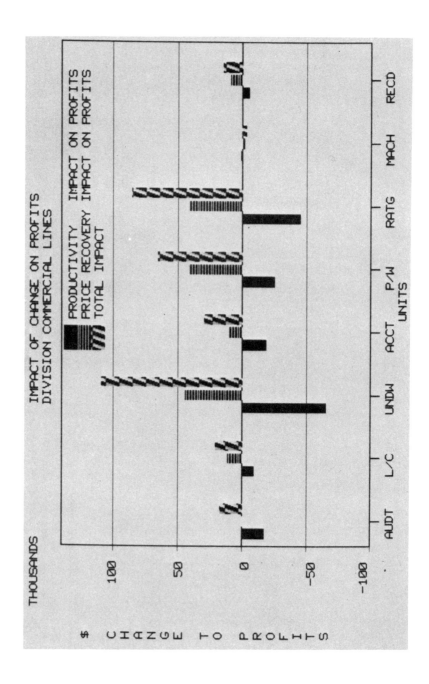

Weighting

Conceptually this is a simple mathematical issue. In the sense of practical application, however, I cannot find the words to describe its complexity adequately. Weighting is simply a matter of taking apples and oranges and converting them to pears.

Weighting implies mill-run generalization, tempered by large numbers and consistency. Weighting does not imply mathematical exactness. If it did, it would not be an issue. Based on certain assumptions, weighting can have an impersonal mathematical expression, as do the theories behind price-weighting. Fairly often—particularly in technical areas—weighting is based on judgment. Whose judgment? The judgment of the involved managers and employees. Therefore, measurement weighting is complex because it invariably involves biased judgment.

It is easy to visualize the corporate political implications of weighting. Productivity programs in your company will have their detractors. To disagree on the weighting principles is to question the measurement results. To question the creditability of the measurement results is to cast doubt on the entire productivity improvement program.

When corporate officers argue over the reliability of the measurement results, the corporate productivity program is relegated to a state of ambiguity. The chief officer usually resolves the dispute against the productivity issue. Why? Because the issue of white collar productivity is new and has not established a firm reputation for itself, a firm political foundation. These are simply words of caution.

What Do You Measure?

The productivity formula is output over input. Input is usually easy to identify for measurement. For input, you should measure the productivity of all the elements that affect your expense ratio. The single expense element of labor cost is emphasized in this text because we are addressing the people-side of the white collar dilemma. You should consider *all* expense elements, however. Total factor productivity should include in the denominator (input) capital, raw materials, and energy costs, as well as labor. An example of the need to consider more than just labor is mechanization or computerization. If you eliminate jobs because of mechanization or computerization, your labor productivity will go up, but at what offsetting cost?

When you measure productivity, you must corral all interrelated expense issues and then display the interrelationship.

It's easy to visualize the input. The output can be a conceptual nightmare. The units involved in the actual corporate output are the easiest to handle. In the insurance industry, it is not hard to visualize policies in force or premium dollars as the output associated with producing insurance policies for the productivity evaluation of employees, computer time, capital, and so on. That's the easy part. Now consider this: what is the output for the marketing department, the maintenance crew, the medical department, or your legal staff? If you want to stir up a political hornet's nest, just suggest that you measure the productivity of your accountants and lawyers.

The nightmare grows as you move your numerator conceptually away from the production units of your corporation. You are in business to produce widgets. You are not in business to produce legal briefs. Yet you may find both indicators used as a measurement of output. I am confident that widgets make productivity sense. I am not confident the same holds true for legal briefs. It is not that legal briefs could not represent productivity output. They could. But they also represent *activity*, and that is the issue. A measurement pitfall occurs when you confuse macromeasurement and micromeasurement. Micromeasurement pertains to activities. As you move away from obvious production indicators for your output, you enter a measurement never-never land. As I said about weighting, at this point you need the input of the involved individuals. If you were they, what would you suggest as a key volume indicator? You would suggest the common activities that you perform.

One problem is that activities can justify staffing rather than indicate proper staffing relationships. The activity pitfall is appealing because the computer usually provides a convenient count. That is another side to the measurement issue. You cannot measure something you cannot count. Therefore, we tend to take established indicators that already provide a count. That could be either an appropriate way to measure or an easy out. Also, activities can be manipulated—the department measured should not have control over the numerator. The fact that the company can become better at performing activities than at producing its product is of little consequence when you consider that it is the product, not the activities, that pays the bills.

MICROMEASUREMENT

Earlier, we talked about the advantage blue collar industries have over white collar industries because they use machines already calibrated at 100 widgets per hour, or 800 widgets per shift. In the white collar industry, we do not have that advantage. We deal with people, not machines, and people do not come calibrated.

Many white collar activities are demonstrable, however, and are therefore measurable. Measurement is critical to the white collar productivity problem and its solution. The 4/8 Theory again comes into play because it is a measure of human activity related to a reasonable expectation of production.

The measurement of human activity raises the specter of the stopwatch. I submit it is not the timing of human activity that should draw criticism. If criticism is appropriate, it should relate to how the information is used.

In any event, if you wish to deal with the issue of white collar productivity, your company must undergo a thorough analysis of all the basic activities performed in the white collar area and then determine how much time it should take to complete each activity. Micromeasurement gives your company the foundation upon which you build your white collar productivity improvement system. Understand, micromeasurement by itself is not a productivity improvement system. In chapter five, I address the various popular productivity improvement systems. At that time, you will see how you can use micromeasurement.

Two Methods of Micromeasurement

Measurement on the micro scale may or may not mean timing individual activities. Two general methods of measurement are in popular use. In both methods, the starting place is the fine analysis of all activities to be performed in any given operation. I said a fine analysis. I meant just that. You must break down all activities into their constituent tasks. Then you must determine the length of time it takes to perform each task. The first way to determine how long it takes to perform an activity is by observation and timing. A productivity consultant can do this accurately, unobtrusively, and without using a stopwatch. The second popular method of determining time is by reducing the activity to its elementary component parts. Then, based on a predetermined scientific method, you construct a time for the entire activity. Either method is satisfactory. The major issue is not the method of measurement, but rather the need to understand accurately what you are measuring.

A word of caution. With the timing of employee activities, you have acquired the basic knowledge to make rate a white collar productivity issue. Don't be lured into that measurement morass.

MEASUREMENT SUMMARY[4]

Not only is measurement the starting place for productivity improvement, but also without it you are in trouble. As a manager, you really do not have the option of either measuring or not measuring.

At this point, you should now understand that measurement falls into two general categories.

First is the macro category that is similar to a corporate, division, or unit report card of productivity progress. For illustrative purposes, I call this the top-down measurement.

Second is the micro category represented by the measurement of individual work tasks. These measured tasks provide the building blocks of your white collar productivity improvement programs. For illustrative purposes, I call this the bottom-up measurement.

Finally, the subtle issue. Measurement does not tell you if your productivity performance is good or bad. It simply gives you a benchmark to progress from. At the outset, we must all assume that our performance is unsatisfactory.

BUDGETING

Budgeting enhancement is a natural byproduct of the macro productivity measurement system. This point can be expressed without becoming unduly complicated. Again, my purpose is simply to introduce the premise.

First, let's discuss the purpose of budgeting. Budgeting is business's attempt, over the short term, to control the future. For business, it is the managed extrapolation of current and past history.

---

[4] For a more detailed development of the subject of measurement and its relationship to strategic planning, see appendix one.

You cannot accurately budget your expenses without knowing your present productivity factors.

You may disagree. After all, you have been budgeting for years without any productivity factors. All I can do at this stage is suggest why your corporate budgets are not being taken seriously after the dust from the approval battles has settled. Your budgets probably do little beyond establishing a policing lid for expenses. Why? Because they are not tied to reality. You need the productivity factor to make that tie.

To see this point in practice, let's examine hypothetical Widget Company One and Widget Company Two, two companies competing with each other in the same market. To start with, let's assume that during the current year both companies are on equal footing. To make it simple, let's also assume that next year is a no-growth year.

There is a seasonal demand for the product sold by both firms. Consequently, their production level varies throughout the year. This cyclical trend in production, the firms' work force counts, and their productivity index are displayed in table 5.

Table 5

CURRENT YEAR—WIDGET COMPANY ONE AND WIDGET COMPANY TWO

Quarters	Units Produced	Actual Work Force	Productivity Index
1ST	264,000	450	586.6
2ND	286,000	450	635.6
3RD	297,000	450	660.0
4TH	253,000	450	562.2
AVERAGE	275,000	450	611.1

Neither company has a productivity measurement system, so neither is aware of the index shown in the rightmost column. Notice that both companies kept their staffing constant at 450 employees, even though their production needs varied. Neither company tracked its cyclical production trend or related this to its work force. Consequently, both companies failed to see the fluctuation in their productivity; in this case, it went from as

72

low as 562 to as high as 660, a 17-percent swing. Their productivity averaged only 611 units produced per employee during the year.

At this point, let's say that Widget Company Two installs a productivity measurement system. The company becomes aware of fluctuations in its productivity level. It realizes that during the third quarter of the current year it was actually capable of producing 660 units per employee. The company also discovers that it has previously staffed for its production peak. Based on this realization, the company forecasts the work force it really requires by planning to maintain productivity at the constant 660 units per employee that it maintained during the third quarter. The analysis is shown in table 6.

Table 6

NEXT YEAR—WIDGET COMPANY TWO

Quarters	Units Produced	Actual Work Force	Productivity Index
1st	264,000	400	660
2nd	286,000	433.3	660
3rd	297,000	450	660
4th	253,000	383.3	660
AVERAGE	275,000	416.65	660

Through this analysis, the company expects to retain a productivity level of 660 by keeping only an average staff of 416.65 employees next year, assuming no growth. This puts Widget Company One at an immediate 8-percent cost of labor disadvantage if it retains its staff of 450 employees.

Let's now suppose that both companies have potentially improved productivity. For purposes of this example, we are going to assume an identical productivity change-ratio of 1.10 (+10 percent) for both companies. This means the ratio of units produced per employee goes up from 611 to 672 for Widget Company One and 660 to 726 for Widget Company Two. But only Company Two is aware of this, through its productivity measurement system. Therefore only Company Two knows that, even though raw production is constant, it can reduce its labor force. In reality, then, only Company Two turns the potential into an actual productivity increase. For Company Two, what used to take 416.65 employees to produce now requires only 379 employees, because of the increase to a 726-widget productivity level.

As a result of these issues, Widget Company One and Widget Company Two formulate their budgets as shown in table 7.

Table 7

WIDGET COMPANY ONE BUDGET

	Current Year	*Next Year*	*Change*
SALES	$70 million	$70 million	0%
WORK FORCE	450	450	0%
AVERAGE WAGE	$15,000	$16,500	+10%
PAYROLL COST	$6.75 million	$7.4 million	+10%
PRODUCTIVITY	Unknown	Unknown	Unknown

WIDGET COMPANY TWO BUDGET

	Current Year	*Next Year*	*Change*
SALES	$70 million	$70 million	0%
WORK FORCE	450	379	−15.8%
AVERAGE WAGE	$15,000	$16,500	+10%
PAYROLL COST	$6.75 million	$6.25 million	−7.4%
PRODUCTIVITY	611 units per employee	726 units per employee	+18.8%

Which company has the better competitive position?

Which company has the more accurate budget?

The unspoken problem is that Company One's labor budget of $7.4 million is probably a self-fulfilling prophecy. Next year, simply by maintaining a constant productivity level, Company Two gains an eight-percent labor-cost advantage. Combined with awareness of improved productivity, the labor-cost gap widens to 18.4 percent. In 10 years, which company is more likely to be driven out of business? That's right. Why? Because Company One did not measure productivity and relate this to historical production trends.

Productivity's Natural Cycles

Earlier I said, "Suppose that both companies have potentially improved productivity." I did not explain why productivity improved. Was that an error? After all, productivity just doesn't improve as the result of a bolt out of the blue.

There is in existence an interesting popular perception: that productivity must constantly be manipulated. As a nation we are so intent on increasing productivity that we lose sight of the fact that every operation experiences natural up and down swings in productivity. Why? Well, one reason I have already cited several times is that trainees become experienced workers who leave and are replaced by trainees. Many reasons are given for the decline in white collar productivity. But the reverse of every reason for a decline is a reason for improvement. If boredom causes productivity to decline, interest causes it to improve.

The topic of this chapter has been measurement and its relationship to productivity improvement. The Catch 22 is that the lack of measurement bears a relationship to declining productivity.

Productivity swings occur naturally in our work environment. Declining productivity takes the control of work out of the hands of the supervisor and places it under the unwitting control of the employee. Here is the Catch 22. When productivity reemerges from the employee, its reemergence cannot be quantified without measurement. Therefore, control cannot be reestablished. How many times have you heard this statement: "We sure got a lot done today." My immediate response is, "Why? Why today? What do you mean by a lot? A lot as opposed to what?" Once you answer these questions, you are well on your way to getting "a lot" done each day: increased productivity.

Again the issue turns back to measurement.

I have often thought that with measurement, quantification, and control, productivity would increase without any formal productivity improvement program. Simply catch each productivity peak. Understand it. Control it. Sustain it. Turn it into the base and await the next peak. But, that still requires measurement and close, competent management control. It also takes time. As I will show, you can orchestrate and capture the peaks.

5

Current White Collar Productivity Improvement Methods

As with toothpaste and soap, hundreds of brands of white collar productivity improvement systems flood the market. The potential consumer should know how these products differ from one another. Most brands of white collar productivity improvement systems are simply variations on a handful of basic themes. In this chapter I shall briefly describe the popular productivity improvement methods currently in use.

MICROMEASUREMENT

I referred to micromeasurement as the building block of a white collar productivity improvement program. Today, three general systems use micromeasurement methods.

1. Employee measurement

2. Monetary reward

3. Short-interval scheduling

As an introduction to the three systems, let's define the following terms.

● **Passive System.** A passive system of productivity improvement is a system that is installed and then *awaits* productivity results.

● **Active System.** An active system of productivity improvement incorporates a method to cause improved productivity as a result of certain techniques.

● **Employee-Intensive System.** An employee-intensive system of productivity improvement places responsibility for the productivity solution on the conscience of the employee.

● **Supervisory-Intensive System.** A supervisory-intensive system of productivity improvement places the productivity solution in the hands of the supervisor.

Three Systems

The three systems we are going to explain are commonly referred to as either "work-management" or "work-measurement." Their installation in a company is usually not accompanied by a great deal of theory on the "why," but always with strong emphasis on the "how to." You can readily see the blue collar origins of these systems. They are based on rate of activity.

The basic underlying methodology for the three systems is very simple. You must get control of the individual employee's productivity performance. Getting control is possible once you know how long it should take an employee to do each and every task assigned to that employee during the workday. As an example, at the end of a 7.25-hour day (net after lunch and breaks), say an employee has completed five hours of assigned measured work. Assuming no unscheduled assignments, that employee performed at a productivity level of 68.97 percent (5 ÷ 7.25).

In most systems of employee measurement, fatigue and delay are factored into the measurement methodology. The result is that often 100 percent equals an average performance. (These systems should not be related to chapters two and three.) As you will see from the following three descriptions, each has its own logic.

1. Employee Measurement

This system entails little management or organizational adjustment. It is based primarily on paper controls. Once the tasks are measured, the employees simply keep track of how many times each day they do each task. (Under certain circumstances, machines do this tracking.) Each employee and/or the supervisor keep track of any time spent in unmeasured or unscheduled activities.

It has been decided in advance how long the employee should take to perform each task. The employee now tracks how many times each task was performed. Someone keeps track of any unscheduled time that the employee spends in meetings, training, etc.

What's the employee's productivity for that day? To find that answer, you need only multiply the tasks performed by the predetermined time allotted to each activity. Then divide that figure by the net hours in the day (the hours available in the day, minus the unscheduled time). The rest is simple. The supervisor deals with each individual employee based on her or his productivity record. Quite often, the productivity records are turned into standings and posted to foster peer pressure or team spirit.

I define this as an employee-intensive passive system. If the system works correctly, the employees deliver increased production. The drawback with this approach is that it places the employee under the gun to solve the company's productivity problem. It clearly says to the employee, "You're the problem because you are not working hard enough." Then management sits back and waits to see if the employees will solve the company's productivity dilemma.

2. Monetary Reward

This is a variation of the employee-measurement system, except in this case a productivity standard is set and bonuses are paid to individuals for exceeding the standard. The amount of the bonus depends on the degree to which the standard was exceeded and the individual's ability to sustain this enhanced level of performance.

This is probably the most passive and employee-intensive system. If this system works correctly, the employees deliver increased production. This approach has the same basic problem as the preceding one. It also implies that paying a bonus is the only way management can get more than four hours of work for eight hours of pay.

I feel I should contrast this approach with quality-of-work-life programs that incorporate an incentive system on a group basis. An incentive system on a group basis eliminates the negative problems of the individual employee reward program and substitutes a positive team approach. If the unit in question has its basic management skills in order (as outlined in chapters six, seven, and eight), the group approach could be a potent tool to further enhance quality and productivity.

3. Short-Interval Scheduling

This system entails a degree of supervisory and organizational adjustment. The supervisor collects and quantifies all the work of a unit in a batching station. The supervisor then batches the work in one-hour groupings and gives it to the employees at one-hour intervals. Since the supervisor expects the work to be done in one hour, the supervisor also checks for the completed batches every hour. Since the interval is short, if the work is not completed at the appointed time, the supervisor can easily review the hour with the employee to determine what problems the employee encountered. Everyone is given the same amount of work, the maximum amount. The work of each employee is recorded and managed, much as in the work-measurement method.

This is a supervisory- and employee-intensive system. It is an active system. When this system works, the employee delivers increased production. The main problem with this system is its obvious concern with rate. Gems of management logic support this approach, such as scheduling work through a unit. Unfortunately this approach falls victim to a "machine loading people" mentality. As a result, employees receive it with mixed emotion. It's safe to say that in its purest form, this system does not have popular support.

In summary, white collar productivity improvement systems that find their productivity expression in a micromeasurement system are the most common. They have obvious strengths and weaknesses. Nevertheless, as I have stated, these systems work when they are properly installed. I should point out that they are far more complex and have far more depth than I've described here. I have given only a brief outline of these alternative methods.

PURSUIT OF POTENTIAL

Macromeasurement is your corporate, division, or firstline unit report card. If you think about macromeasurement in that sense, you can almost visualize a productivity improvement system. After all, what is the driving force behind a report card? It is the fact that you are being compared.

I call this approach "Pursuit of Potential." The one unique ingredient this approach needs is multiple, common units, because the foundation of the approach is competition. This approach is also universal. It works equally well in a blue collar situation as in a white collar situation.

The basic premise is the ability to measure the productivity of common units. As you will recall, I said a single productivity measure tells you very little. By itself it does not tell you whether you are below or above average. But, let's say you have 10 common units and, therefore, 10 individual productivity results. Why not take the 10 individual productivity results and, since the units are similar, strike an average? You still don't know—nor will you ever know—if that average represents poor, average, or good productivity. You do know that you want improvement, however, and the macromeasuring system gives you the ability to track this improvement.

We make an assumption.

All units falling below average need to catch up.

All units above average set the productivity standard.

Who wants the president to feel that his or her unit's performance is below standard? The below average units pursue the track records demonstrated by the above average units. The above average units can't relax because the improvement efforts of the problem units are raising the average.

The result: productivity must rise.

This is a passive method that is neither employee- nor supervisory-intensive. You might say that it is manager- or vice president-intensive. You develop a strong one-two punch by marrying this Pursuit of Potential macro system to a micro system.

MECHANIZATION AND COMPUTERIZATION

As you read this book, the one question that must keep coming to mind is, "When is he going to say something about how to use computers, word processors, machine enhancements in general to solve productivity problems?"

My answer is simple: I'm not.

The huge void in white collar productivity is not the lack of electronic and mechanical help. In fact, the biggest boon to these aids is the fact that we have failed to deal adequately with the human side of productivity. The general feeling seems to be that if we can't get satisfactory production out of an employee group, we should replace it with a machine. I grant logic says that any group of people, no matter how efficient, could conceivably be replaced by a more productive machine. We turn to that alternative too quickly, however. We do not tackle the really tough job of optimizing our employee productivity first. At worst, this rush to mechanical alternatives can do our corporations a costly injustice. At best it can be misleading.

Investment in a mechanized alternative is often cost-justified based on the savings it will bring about in the supporting payroll. But how accurate is that cost justification when it is based on a payroll that is only 50-percent efficient? These cost-effectiveness studies usually assume that the productivity of the supporting payroll is as efficient as management can deliver.

Let me explain this last comment with a couple of examples:

1. As you are well aware, insurance companies are heavily dependent on paper. Thus, one processing division decided to microfilm its paper files. A cost-effectiveness study estimated that the conversion to paperless processing would save 14.5 people and have a payback period of 9 months.

After the study, but before its installation, we installed a productivity improvement system. With the installation of the system, a large portion of the payroll savings that microfilming was to achieve were realized. The actual employee savings from microfilming were 6.5 people, and the payback period doubled to 18 months.

The company still considered this particular microfilming program cost-effective, but admittedly the underlying considerations had changed.

2. An 11-office processing operation was functioning at a productivity level of 800 transactions per month per employee. In one of these offices, we installed one of our early productivity improvement programs. After the installation, that particular office operated at a productivity level of 1,100 transactions per month per employee.

All 11 offices were converted, at considerable cost, from a keypunch to a CRT operation. The result was that the entire operation went to 1,100 transactions per employee, or to the productivity level of the office with the productivity improvement program.

The CRT's were a sound investment because, when a refined productivity improvement program was installed in all 11 offices, the overall productivity level went up substantially.

The point is that you can only accurately determine the cost-effectiveness of mechanized and computerized alternatives when you are operating from a sound employee productivity base.

QUALITY-OF-WORK-LIFE

I don't have too much to say about quality-of-work-life, except that it can be a very effective approach in addressing the issues of quality and productivity. Besides, the quality of an employee's work-life presents a rather obvious moral obligation to a company, quite apart from profit considerations.

Again I emphasize that immediate, durable productivity improvement can be achieved when management finally realizes the extent of white collar waste within its own company offices. We need to improve our management style. But, however much the lack of management basics may be at fault, we should not ignore the parallel issue—management's inattention to employee quality-of-work-life. We must also devote immediate attention to this if we hope to improve productivity to an optimal level. The two issues are not mutually exclusive.

Effective supervision is important. Returning to the basic, common sense elements of good management is important. It takes a sound management foundation to promote a quality-of-work-life program successfully. A company has to start with strong internal control before it can orchestrate creative management elasticity.

Finally, don't be misled by my lopsided stress of the less personal side of productivity improvement. The press is already giving quality-of-work-life a great deal of exposure. Volumes upon volumes have been written on the subject. You should give these texts thoughtful attention. Because these texts are available, however, I shall not discuss participative management in general or approaches such as suggestion systems in particular. I shall, however, spend a few paragraphs on quality circles.

Quality Circles

Let's start this discussion by examining the term "quality circles." The concept originated in the Japanese industrial community as an answer to the quality problems Japan faced after World War II. Today, the United States has embraced the concept as one approach to solving our national productivity and quality problems. The crossover from quality to productivity is a natural bridge. The central issue of improved productivity cannot exist apart from the quality factor. Having to do things twice because they were not done right the first time is hardly conducive to productivity. Or, how productive is it to produce an abundance of goods that consumers soon learn to mistrust and stop buying?

The name quality circle is insignificant. Its allure stems from its Japanese origin. We now buy anything stamped "Made in Japan." The good news is that the purchases are often quality products and quality ideas. The bad news for the United States is that the products and ideas are those of a competitor.

So much has been written on the subject of quality circles that I need not define the premise. I am simply going to give you my opinion as to the proper positioning of quality circles in a white collar productivity improvement program.

First, realize that quality circles work when properly positioned. Their basic premise is so logical that it is hard to believe that they could not work. What do I mean, "work"? I mean that they will live up to your reasonable expectations. You can initially pay as much as $5,000 to $10,000 to establish a quality circle. Obviously, you can also pay almost nothing. The adage that you get what you pay for also applies to quality circles. Many, maybe most, quality circles are never measured. But when they are, the results are usually reported as a return on investment. If you expect to recover several times your investment, I don't think you will be disappointed.

Quality circles are obviously a passive technique that is neither employee- nor supervisory-intensive.

The issue is at what point you get quality circles involved in your white collar productivity improvement program. The most carefully devised quality circles, by themselves, do not constitute a white collar productivity improvement program. At best, they are only an element within such a program.

Quality circles have been readily assimilated into the manufacturing area. This is understandable when you consider that in respect to the state of the art in productivity, the manufacturing sector is far ahead of U.S. white collar industries. As an aside, if manufacturing is so far ahead of the white collar industries, why is the United States still faced with a productivity problem in the manufacturing sector? I don't say the manufacturing sector has solved its problem. But, the problem confronting heavy industry in America has nothing to do with knowing how many widgets its machines will produce. Manufacturers know. And they know it is not enough.

American manufacturers face the problem of accumulating the capital to either buy or develop a breakthrough generation of widget-making machines. By now, it must be clear that the problems of blue collar productivity differ drastically and demand different solutions from the problems of white collar productivity. The basic reason for this is that blue collar and white collar productivity improvement systems are at different stages of development. Therefore, quality circles may have more influence on productivity today in the blue collar sector than in the white collar sector.

Quality circles and suggestion programs are an integral part of a comprehensive white collar productivity improvement program. When placed in priority order, they become a consideration after macromeasurement has begun and a micromeasurement system has been developed. Quality circles are the icing on the productivity cake. Don't confuse them with the cake. As positive as I am on the issue of quality circles, I am going to end this section on a contrary note. The following is not a firm conclusion, it is more food for thought, a question.

Do quality circles fit in the workaday world of the knowledge worker? I'm not sure. The knowledge worker is paid to spend a substantial portion of the day thinking, being creative. You can take individuals off the production line or out of the clerical process and place them in a quality circle and say, "Give us some creativity." You can do that because they are not paid to be creative in their daily lives. Therefore, a quality circle can work well in their situation. Take groups of attorneys, accountants, and engineers, however, and say to them, "We want you to form quality circles so we can tap your creativity." That statement is either a redundancy or an acknowledgment of failure. Even so, I can see a quality circle working with the knowledge worker, because knowledge workers, though they may sit together, often work in creative isolation. Do quality circles speak to this last point? Or do basic management techniques? I feel it is the latter. Invariably, as I mull through the issue of productivity improvement systems, the road home always leads to management.

6

An Approach

The real cause of America's present white collar productivity problem is management, not labor. We can solve this dilemma of white collar waste. The solution is not an exotic theory. The solution is to return to basic management principles.

I wish to emphasize that last point. White collar productivity can be increased simply by systematically returning working units to basic management principles. It's that simple. Whenever I approach a new assignment, clients invariably want to refer to our back-to-basics approach as "my system," as if I invented organization, planning, execution, and control. Then, after I leave the client unit, they say, "Your system works."

Are we so far from the management basics that they appear refreshingly new?

As I discuss the approach we use, keep in mind it is not a new theory; it is not exotic. Therefore, it is not in conflict with any of the popular quality-of-work-life theories. Would anyone say that the expression of quality-of-work-life conflicts with organization, planning, execution, and control?

As a nation, we have heavily concerned ourselves with the quality-of-work-life as it affects productivity. As I stated in chapter five, this issue is very real and needs immediate attention. We need to approach the productivity problem on parallel tracks, however. Management can cause immediate, significant, and durable productivity improvement results. To improve the quality-of-work-life requires a longer time frame.

Am I pitching organization, planning, execution, and control for the sake of organization, planning, execution, and control? No. I have simply found that, when you understand the basic principles of white collar efficiency, you realize that the solution to the productivity problem lies in a back-to-management-basics approach. What are the basic principles of white collar efficiency?

A.   White collar waste is intangible.

B.   American white collar employees today work four hours out of every eight on the job.

C.   Excess worker capacity exists today.

D.   To solve our productivity problems, we must make efficient use of each employee's day.

E.   Because the problem is not the employee, the solution is not

    1.   rate,

    2.   the work ethic, or

    3.   the new generation.

F.   The problem . . . and the solution . . . lie with management.

These are simple concepts, but how do you apply them to an organization of 1, 10, 50, or 100,000 employees? How do you change the management and supervisory style of 50, 100, 1000, or 10,000 managers and supervisors? When you consider the nature and magnitude of the problem, an obvious answer rushes to mind: training. Though that sounds logical, it is not the answer. It is simply not practical to take a supervisory staff of hundreds or thousands, whose individual members are in their positions by virtue of seniority and technical skills, and train them to be consummate experts on organization, planning, execution, and control.

The Work Unit—Management's Neglected Area

To complicate this issue, white collar industries have neglected a basic area of management. On the whole, we have failed to organize the basic white collar work unit. We meticulously organize work to and from units. We develop elaborate workflow charts that give the impression of organization. The problem is in what the workflow charts do not show. They don't show how the work flows once it is in the unit. The usual answer to that is, "Well, that's the supervisors' problem. That's what we pay them for."

Is that so?

Let's look at a typical white collar supervisor in a typical white collar unit. I am going to burlesque this description. Therefore, take it illustratively, not literally.

Let's start with dependable Mary, our supervisor. What do we pay Mary to do? Mary has 10 employees working under her. Her unit receives 800 paper widgets to be screened, analyzed, and computed. The widgets must proceed through three stations within her unit. She is our certified expert, so she has the job of organizing this procedure. Remember, it is management's responsibility to organize the flow of widgets to her unit and from her unit.

Before we look at Mary's organizing skill, let's look at her background for this management assignment. Ten years ago, Mary quit high school in the middle of her junior year to go to work at Widget Paper, Inc. She had to go to work to support her husband, Joe, who wanted to continue his education and complete high school. After Joe was expelled and went to work in the town mill, they bought a little house. Mary was going to have a baby and wanted to quit her job. The little house needed new carpeting, however, so Mary opted for maternity leave. Two more babies came along. The carpet was paid for, but now Mary and Joe needed a new car. Mary had never been thrilled with working at Widget Paper, Inc., but it's been just one thing after another. Now she has been with the company seven years. She is the senior employee in the unit and the only employee with a thorough understanding of widget computing. Furthermore—and this is a key point—she is the only employee who knows how to track down a lost widget.

Mary's unit supervisor quits. The question now is who to choose as a successor to this title, the $35 raise, and the honor of the desk with the side chair.

The solution is obvious.

What does Mary do? She takes the promotion and becomes a career employee.

The basic white collar management omission that I mentioned earlier is that management has historically dropped the ball once the work was organized and channeled to the unit. Once the work is in the unit, it is up to the supervisor to process it.

How does Mary carry out her supervisory chores? Baskets of paper widgets are delivered to her unit at various periods throughout the day. They are dropped off at the desks of the screening employees. They, in turn, do their job and then put the widgets in their out baskets, which they place on a table when full. The analyzing employees periodically pick up the baskets and take them to their desks. When these employees are finished, they put the widgets on another table and the computing employees pick them up, and so on until the work is fully processed.

No scheduling problems have ever shown up, because employees always have plenty of work in progress . . . backlog. What does Mary do? Mary handles all the tough problems, performs her search specialty, and pitches in to clear work bottlenecks.

If this scenario sounds familiar, then consider the fact that a major portion of your company's employees fall under the direct supervision of these reluctant leaders who, I should add, do the best they can with what little management help the company gives them.

We owe the supervisor more than just help or training; we owe the supervisor a system. The system should enable supervisors to accomplish their job in the most timely and productive manner possible. If you think about this a minute, it is a common approach in manufacturing. The general manager of the Widget Manufacturing Company would not say to the foreman, "Here's the raw material, here's the manual, there are the workbenches, and there are the people: Go make widgets." On the contrary, that general manager would have industrial engineers design a step-by-step production line that would lead to the timely, quality output of a desired number of widgets. The engineers would then take the foreman and say, "Here's the system; see that it runs."

What we do in the service industry is more analogous to choosing a sandlot football coach. We take the player who knows the rules and can do the best job of running, tackling, and passing. We say, "There's the field, there's the ball, there's the equipment; give us a winning season."

What we get is sandlot processing.

And whose fault is that? Not the supervisors'.

Supervisors are naturally and normally inclined to do the best with what they have. The problem is with middle and top management. They are the ones who should solve the problem of declining productivity.

A Return to Basic Management Principles

In the 4/8 Theory lies the opportunity to improve productivity. Originally, the 4/8 Theory seemed to me to be analogous to a known but remote reservoir of oil. It simply was awaiting the technical development needed to tap its riches.

As I thought on this subject, however, the elusive answer lost its elusiveness. We don't need new and mysterious techniques. In fact, as I have repeated several times, the answer lies in the basic management approaches we have always known. We not only failed to avail ourselves of the answer; but also, we could not see it for the trees.

Think through this situation with me: White collar efficiency is low (50 percent) because the average employee gives us only 30 minutes of effort over 60 elapsed minutes. A reasonable efficiency level to expect is 75 percent, which means increasing the efficiency effort to 45 minutes for an elapsed 60-minute period. The answer is not to cause anyone to work faster. The answer is to have the employee work more consistently. This is a reasonable request to which the average employee is willing to respond. Therefore, we must place the issue of efficient use of the day within the control of the supervisor (firstline management).

How To Build a Solution

If you as a supervisor were faced with the issue of how to use the day efficiently and relied on current management techniques, how would you build a system to solve the problem? In aggressively solving a problem, it is essential to assume from the start that you are going to cause the solution to occur.

What are we dealing with? We are dealing with people and tasks. We are dealing with a workday.

Then, according to my statement, we are going to cause the employees to use the workday efficiently. We are going to make it happen. That is such a simple statement it sounds silly. But think about the average white collar operation today. Isn't the average operation one that tracks results instead of causing them? How often is work assessed by waiting until 5 p.m., until Friday, or, worse yet, until the end of the month to say, "Well, where are we? How's it going?"

94

If you want to rid your company of white collar waste, you must make the day occur, the week occur, and the month occur. If your task is to make the day occur, it does no good to wait till 5 p.m. to see what happened.

How do you make a workday occur?

1) By organizing it.

2) By planning it.

3) By executing it.

4) By controlling it.

If you follow these four basic principles, you will provide quality service in a timely manner by maintaining a smooth and consistent flow of work through each employee station—increased efficiency.

How do you do it? Not by training the supervisor to be the consummate manager. Instead, you owe the supervisor a system. You need to fulfill management's obligation to the supervisor and bring organization to the unit. You must orchestrate a smooth and consistent workflow.

But you can't move something smoothly and consistently if you do not have control over it. In this case, "it" is the work. Mary was a good example of this point. In her unit, all work flowed from employee to employee. The work never found its way to Mary unless it was a problem. If, at the beginning of any given workday, a supervisor views the unit's work as being on desks, in desks, in sideboards, on tables, in mail bags, in file cabinets, etc., how can that supervisor control the work smoothly and consistently?

The supervisor has to have physical control over the work. Earlier, I used the term "basic management approaches." We can't get much more basic than this. Let's assume that the supervisor now has physical control over the work.

It's no good simply to say, "The work." If the unit's tasks are to be moved smoothly and consistently, you really need to know what the tasks are. You must give some thought to your priorities, resources, training levels, experience levels, etc. What you need, in sum, is a plan. Remember, rate is not an issue. The issue is the efficient utilization of each employee's day. Implicit in that statement is the issue of planning.

Since our thought process is operating at a rather basic level, let me explain how you could construct a clerical system. I shall use the same approach as we use in a real situation to explain this concept to firstline supervisors. We do this in scenario form through a dialogue between a line manager and a supervisor. At this point, we have already explained the efficient use of the day as the foundation (4/8) for productivity improvement. The manager is now discussing with the supervisor the tools and techniques to execute the theory.

TIME: Late afternoon.

Manager. I would like you to plan tomorrow's workday for your employees.

Supervisor. What?

Manager. What I mean is, tomorrow I want you in control of the efficient use of your unit's workday.
Make the day happen!

Supervisor. (Silence)

Manager. What do you need to know to plan your day?

Supervisor. A lot of things.

Manager. Would you need to know where all your work is?

Supervisor. I suppose so.

Manager. Where is the work right now?

Supervisor. Some of it's on the desks.
Some of it's in the desks.
Some of it's in the broadsides.
Some of it's on that table over there.
A lot of it's on my desk.
Some of it's lost.

Manager. Let's gather all that work and place it on this table.

Supervisor. (In stunned silence the supervisor gathers all the work and heaps it on the table.)

96

Manager. To plan your work, you need to know where it is.

Supervisor. That makes sense.

Manager. Now that we know where the work is, we need to know how much work there is. How much is there?

Supervisor. That much. (Pointing to the table)

Manager. How much is that much?

Supervisor. A lot.

Manager. How much is a lot?

Supervisor. Plenty.

Manager. Well, now we know where the work is and we know you have plenty of it. How do we know where it goes?

Supervisor. Where is goes? It goes where it was. When it was where it was, I knew where it was. With it stacked up here, I don't know where it goes unless I look at each piece of work and sort it out.

Manager. Let's look at each piece and sort it out.

Supervisor. (The supervisor sorts out the work.)

Manager. Now we've got it all sorted out. So now we know what we've got and where it is. How long will it take to do it?

Supervisor. All day and then some.

Manager. How many hours will it take?

Supervisor. How many hours? If I knew that I'd be the world's greatest guesser.

Manager. You don't need to guess. I can tell you how to figure it out for yourself in just a few minutes. Do you want to know?

Supervisor. Beautiful. You had me stack and sort this work. I was hoping that there would be a good reason for it.

Manager.   The key is in how long it will take to do each stack of tasks.

Supervisor.   I won't know that unless I know how long it takes to do each task.

Manager.   What if I told you I had determined the length of time to do each task?

Supervisor.   Okay. Give me a piece of scratch paper, and I'll multiply the time it takes for each task times the number of individual tasks. I guess that will tell us how much work we have.

Manager.   Great, except I've got a preprinted planning sheet here with all the tasks listed and the times already printed on the sheet. All you have to do is count, fill in the numbers, and multiply.

Supervisor.   Did you invent sliced bread?

Manager.   Now that you've completed that part of your planning sheet, you know how many hours your unit needs to get its work done.

Supervisor.   I'm not sure that I do. You know, people do go to the bathroom, think, stretch, look out the windows. Also, some aren't as well-trained as others.

Manager.   You're right. We don't expect any unit to work at 100-percent efficiency. I suggest that you start with a 60-percent efficiency estimate. You do that by dividing the number of hours needed by .60; that will give you your required hours to do the work. Then, as the days and weeks go by, you will soon learn what the real expectation percentage is for your unit and you will then start using that percentage.

Supervisor.   Then, as you said, this planning deal doesn't force my people to work harder or faster.

Manager.   That's right. But what it does do is cause a constant flow of work to pass through your unit.

This eliminates the lost time and activity that goes on when work is not planned.

Supervisor. I've got a problem.

Manager. What's that?

Supervisor. I know how much work I've got, but I won't know until the morning how many people will show up.

Manager. You're catching on. You cannot finish your planning until your people come to work. This will allow you to match your available work-hours—the people that show up—against the required hours to do the work.

Supervisor. How can I plan tomorrow today if I don't know what will be in the next morning's mail?

Manager. In most cases the work that comes in today will be the next day's work, but there are exceptions, such as cash receipts.

Manager. When you plan to control your workday, you find that it stops controlling you. Consequently, you plan to become current and then you plan to stay current. You will be so current that if you don't save today's incoming mail for tomorrow, you will have nothing for your people to do when they come in each morning.
Remember that one problem you face today is that you are being organized by your backlog.
Your backlog plans you.
We will plan your backlog out of existence.

Supervisor. I'll believe that when I see it.

Manager. It will happen.

Supervisor. If I have no backlog, what do I do when I've got more people than work? And how about the work rushes that aren't in my department, but are in other departments on the way to me.

Manager. I guess we need an early morning planning meeting at which all the supervisors can get together and exchange ideas, share people, and jointly plan the day.

Supervisor. Sounds great. For the first time I'll know what I've got, where it's at, and my priorities. Hey, wait a minute! Do I have to do all this counting and prioritizing myself? I'll have no time to supervise.

Manager. You can appoint a helper for the gathering, counting, and prioritizing. This helper should be that person you are training as your backup for vacations and such. You mentioned that you won't have time for supervising. From now on, planning and making your unit's day happen is your main supervisory function.

Supervisor. Yes, but what about all the problems I handle?

Manager. You'll train your employees and assign the problems to them.

Supervisor. No way! I'm the only one capable of handling the tough problems.

Manager. What if you got hit by a truck tonight?

Supervisor. A truck?

Manager. A big truck. Would the problems get handled tomorrow?

Supervisor. I guess they'd have to be. But, what if we get behind? As a supervisor, I always pitch in and help. Will I have time to do that?

Manager. As I mentioned earlier, in your new supervisory role you plan your work so that you are always current. If you get behind, plan your way out of it. Remember, you will be working as a team with the other supervisors.

Supervisor. Okay. There are the people, and here's the work; but how can I make anything happen with people coming up here and picking up work that they may not know how to do? Some may pick up too much work. More than likely, most won't pick up enough. I won't know who's got what. How can I be responsible for making the day happen when I don't have control of the work during the day?

Manager. Well, you have control of the work. It's right here. You know what's here, how much is here, and the priorities. You also know who is sitting out there. You know their interests, abilities, training levels, and so on. You'll have to take this work and match it to the people and hand it out to them.

Supervisor. I agree with everything you've said, except . . . people don't like to have work handed to them. They like to do their own thing.

Manager. For some people you are right. Most people, however, respond to a leader. In battle, who would respond to a leader who commanded, "Those who wish, may charge!"

Supervisor. I get the point. I personally like to work for people I have faith in and who know what they are doing. But most people like to control their own work.

Manager. How big is your family?

Supervisor. Six, including myself.

Manager. I suppose no one's in charge at your place? Everyone does his or her own thing? They all control their own lives?

Supervisor. Are you crazy? That would be a calamity!

Manager. A company is a large family, often with hundreds of family members. A company family also has to pull together to avoid calamity.

Supervisor. You're right. If I'm responsible for making the day happen, then I have to control the work through my unit.

Manager. We are going to give your employees control over one portion of their day.

Supervisor. I'm sold on controlling my day. This isn't going to change that, is it?

Manager. No, in fact it should help. To distribute the work, you will have to hand it out in some fashion. As a guide, we have the rule that the work has to be handed out at least twice a day.

Supervisor. Twice a day or more often if I think it's necessary.

Manager. Yes, but there is one additional rule.

Supervisor. There always is!

Manager. When you hand out work, always include a white ticket on it explaining who got what and when. When you hand out the last work of the day, put a green ticket on it. When they see the green ticket, your employees will know that they can go home as soon as they finish, even if it's way before quitting time. They will get full pay, too. The only exception will be if you develop a formal plan for an employee as a result of the early morning planning meeting. And that exception holds only if you communicate that plan to the employee.

Supervisor. Boy! This is a really new and different approach. You missed another exception. If we have backlog in the department, no one will go home early.

Manager. Oh yes they will! When you've given them the last work assignment and have nothing else planned, then they go home, backlog or not!

Supervisor. (Thinking)

Manager. Does that make sense?

Supervisor. I get the point. You really are serious when you say I have to plan the day. If I don't pay attention to what I'm doing, I could have hours of backlog and everyone going home at 3:00.

102

Manager. You're right. We are serious when we say we want you to plan the day.

Supervisor. That makes sense. I know I'm not to handle problems any more, but when am I going to have time to handle my employees' problems?

Manager. They should put problems aside as they run across them in the work you hand to them. Then, when you follow up on your employees' progress, you can discuss and help them with the problems. They can also come straight to you with any rush problems.

Supervisor. I have to follow up on their work, too.

Manager. Yes, that way you'll keep the work flowing and contact employees several times a day to help them with their problems.

Supervisor. This changes my whole supervisory life. I now know what I've got, where it goes, and how it gets there. I'm really in charge. I control the work—it won't control me any more.

That scenario explains the simple essence of a systematic approach to good unit management. The supervisor still must think and solve problems. But, we have set up a system within which the supervisor functions. The supervisor has a roadmap that each day leads to the proper conclusions. This roadmap also leads to a smooth and consistent workflow.

The scenario was designed to serve as a quick, basic overview. By integrating these management procedures into your productivity improvement system, you produce a system that is:

- supervisory-intensive,
- active, and
- based on micromeasurement.

The scenario also raises certain issues that need to be explained in greater detail:

- micromeasurement program methodology,
- the planning meeting concept, and
- execution.

In the next chapter I shall address these issues.

The important point to understand is that the efficient use of each employee's day is now in the hands of the supervisor. Doesn't this approach also give the supervisor access to the lever of rate? The answer is "No" as long as management stays on top of the program and sees that *the work that is distributed matches realistically the ability of the receiving employee.* Remember, corporate productivity does not concern itself with the underachieving employee. That is, as it always has been, a supervisor-employee issue. As you will see in the next chapter, a planning meeting is at the heart of this approach. Its lifeblood is the shared and coordinated activities of a team of supervisors.

7

The Supervisor's Role

I am not going to turn this text into a primer on basic management. Everyone reading this should have an intuitive feel for the logic and principles underlying organization, planning, execution, and control. In the last chapter, I approached the subject of clerical organization in a very elementary fashion. Now I should like to turn your attention to the variations on the management themes that are necessary to tailor the subject to the issue of improving white collar efficiency.

MICROMEASUREMENT

In all the traditional methods, companies use micromeasurement systems to stimulate individual employees to increase productivity. The systems are employee-intensive.

As I said in chapter six, I view micromeasurement as a planning tool crucial in making the workday happen. I have no interest in using measurement to pressure the individual employee to produce more, only to wait to see if it happens and to what degree. As has been said a number of times, the ability of an individual employee to produce is a product of training and experience. It is management's job to bring productivity sense to the unit. We must develop sensible management procedures and install them. We must bring our supervisors to see the enhancement of productivity as tangible, manageable reality.

Micromeasurement, a Planning Tool

I use a micromeasurement system as a planning tool and as a guide to execute the plan. As in all micromeasurement systems, all tasks are broken into their basic manageable components. Then the unit's most competent employees perform these tasks for the purpose of measurement. The measurements are not adjusted for fatigue and delay, since they will not be used to track individual employees.

If you want an accurate plan, you want a realistic measurement. Therefore, realize that you can't use the measurements in their raw form. Why? Because they represent a 100-percent, machine-like effort, and you are not dealing with machines. You need realistic information to plan accurately.

To get a realistic measurement, take the total measured time and alter it by a planning factor. For example, if a given unit needs 1,000 hours to complete a day's work and we know that the unit is working at 60-percent efficiency, divide the 1,000 hours by a planning factor of .6. This tells you that you need 1,666 employee-hours to make the day happen. The supervisor tracks the planning factor and adjusts it up or down as the situation dictates.

Individual Efficiency Is a Supervisor Issue

As you can well imagine, the micromeasurement system gives supervisors the ability to interpret the efficiency levels of

across the country, the company was running out of plant capacity. The company had planned for growth but never in the range of 250 percent to 300 percent; and it had never expected it to happen so quickly.

Our primary charge was not to increase productivity but to increase the usable life of the plant facilities. Of course, the punchline is that they were one and the same. The strain visible at the end of the first 12 months of growth was totally eliminated, and, as a result, the life of the facilities and equipment was extended by 36 months.

The happiest result was that the company's total cost of doing business dropped more than 15 percent. Dollar output had gone up dramatically, while total expense initially dipped then rose slightly and stabilized.

Increasing white collar productivity means more than dealing with a people-capacity issue. It is also critically related to plant facility requirements. A solid white collar productivity improvement system can significantly reduce a company's need for office space.

THE PLANNING MEETING

Implicit in our back-to-basics approach is planning. To plan, you must be able to quantify the work in the unit; in micromeasurement you have the tools for that purpose. To quantify the work, you must also get physical control over it. Obviously, you must gather the work into one place, count it, and sort it before you can quantify it into hours of work.

In each unit, we establish a supervisory work area: a convenient layout of tables and file cabinets that acts as a work and holding area for the supervisor. To aid the sorting process, the work is substantially labeled by task.

Why do we have to go to all this trouble?

We have the work assembled, counted, placed in priority order, and quantified into employee-hours. Our goal is to get that work off the table and distributed to the employees in a logical, reasonable, consistent, and smooth manner. This doesn't just happen, however, unless you give the process a great deal of thought. For example, do we have more work than people or more people than work? Either way, we have a problem to consider. Do we have a mathematical match of hours to be accomplished and hours available, but a training and experience level that is not equal to the task? It is possible to lack certain critical skills on a given day and still have a mathematical match of hours.

I am driving at an important point: if you wish to orchestrate a workday, then you must score (plan) it.

The Importance of Planning

Most planning issues that apply within a unit also apply among units. The planning task becomes more complicated when you consider that all units in a department must coordinate their plans. You need this coordination for a number of reasons:

1. Work flows erratically through a unit. Units may have heavy and light months; heavy and light weeks within a month; heavy and light days within a week; and, finally, heavy and light hours within a day.

2. Employee count within a unit is erratic. Sick days are totally uncontrollable. Vacation time is predictable, but only in a limited sense.

3. We cannot even rely on skill level. Depending upon turnover, a unit can go through periods of high-skill level, low-skill level, or a balance of high and low levels, none of which you can accurately predict.

4. Employee motivation is another problem. Do employees come to work every day uniformly motivated to respond to

110

supervision and their workload? On the best of days, are they uniformly motivated throughout the day? Some individuals are morning people, while others don't really begin to get their act together until the afternoon.

Are we making a point for planning? Are we making a point for the intangibleness of white collar waste?

If you take all these variations and throw them at an office each day, you can appreciate that even a properly staffed unit today may be understaffed or overstaffed tomorrow. For these reasons, each day all units must come together with their daily plans and coordinate their efforts. Even with two units, you can somewhat mitigate staffing irregularities. With numerous units, you can completely eliminate them.

Think about these questions:

- Do you agree with the examples of workflow/staffing irregularities?

- Do you insist your supervisors deliver quality, timely service?

- Do you ignore planning and the exchange of interunit personnel?

If you answer yes to those questions, then what tool have you forced your supervisors to rely upon to operate their units satisfactorily? The answer is overstaffing, or staffing for peaks. What, then, is the state of your productivity?

Low!

The Meeting

The daily planning meeting does much more than just provide a format for the exchange of personnel among units. It also:

1. Provides an opportunity to exchange information among units about work proceeding in and out of the units.

2. Identifies interunit rush items and high priority items.

3. Fosters the process of problem-solving. Have you ever wondered why certain problems can exist in perpetuity in a given work atmosphere? The answer is the ingrained attitude that usually is expressed in the comment, "Okay, don't worry about it. It's always been that way." Group problem-solving helps the entire organization. Isn't that the focus of quality circles as well as other group methods? Create an atmosphere conducive to a group synergistic experience. Place in this atmosphere the employees with the expertise and technical savvy to solve the anticipated problems.

4. Creates a forum for allowing supervisors to blow off steam. Without a communication forum, emotions, resentments, misunderstandings, gossip, and low morale can all build up.

I think I have made a telling point for the planning meeting. Even though we understand the need, it is sometimes difficult to get the team work and the synergism to take hold. To help establish this synergism, we have come up with a "prime" meeting catalyst and two "secondary" catalysts.

Planning Catalysts

1. *Primary Catalyst.* Goal-setting. The meeting has to have a self-driving purpose. Without such a purpose, the meeting becomes artificial. You must give it a goal.

The goal should be to complete all the work in the department by a certain day and time—to make the day happen. An obvious weekly goal is to be current by 4:30 p.m. on Friday. Because this is obvious, it may be a *complacent* goal. The goal must be flexible. On a light week it could be to become current by Thursday at 4:30 p.m. and to whip Friday off by noon.

The goal must constantly test everyone's ability to plan, or the planning process will become so routine it will disappear, and productivity will decline. To plan to reach a weekly goal, the supervisors have to plan daily goals. As in the case of the weekly goal, the daily goal must always stretch the supervisors' imagination and planning ability.

On a heavy Monday when there is more work than people, the supervisor sets the priorities and plans to have a predetermined portion of that day's work done by 4:30 p.m. The unit may not work out the results of a heavy Monday until Wednesday at 4:30. On Thursday, the reverse may happen. Thursday may be light. In that case, the supervisor plans to complete Thursday by 3 p.m.

Remember:

- Don't wait until the end of the day to see how the day went.
- Don't wait until the end of the week to see how the week went.
- Make the day happen.
- Make the week happen.

2. *Secondary Catalysts.*

a. Exchanging People. If work flows through a unit based on an hourly, daily, weekly, monthly, and annual cycle; if employee attendance is not totally dependable; if individual skill levels fluctuate; if you can't count on the motivation of individual employees, units will probably have mismatches of available people-hours and available work. The answer to that problem is to have a mechanism to exchange people across unit lines. This is a must. Supervisors will pick up on this need in the planning meeting. It is so natural that quite often this becomes the sole purpose of the meeting. If that happens, in a few months the supervisors will realize they can exchange people without a meeting, and the planning process dies. Then, by the end of the first year, the people exchange drops off and so does productivity.

The exchange of people is a hot item in the meeting. It must remain a hot item. It must remain in the meeting. Exchanging people also drives another office discipline that companies always acknowledge as important but then seldom really work at—cross-training. This is probably the most

113

people-oriented portion of the program. It provides the opportunity to make the job more interesting and also to broaden and develop an employee's career.

b. Problem-solving. As you identify a department's problems, assign them to teams of supervisors. Devote part of each daily meeting to team reports on progress and solutions.

The primary and secondary catalysts, as indicated, help get the synergism to take hold. The force that puts the process in gear, however, is the meeting leader. This person, vested with the proper authority to lead the individual functions to achieve office-wide goals provides the crucial managerial control for the planning process.

The leader reviews individual unit plans before the morning meeting. He or she may change those plans as required to ensure office-wide consistency in the planning process and keep all the individual units on the same track.

This individual is responsible to top management for executing the office-wide plan and achieving the goal. With these tools, along with management's constant and intense interest as expressed by and through the meeting leader, the meetings will stay alive and the system will continue to maintain and enhance productivity.

Two Meeting Byproducts

1. Every hour in the business day is important, but the first three hours of the business day are the most important. The first part of the day sets the tone for the entire day. The planning process and the meetings instill, in the opening hours of every day, a sense of production urgency. This is an enormous benefit in and of itself.

2. The planning meeting provides a unique opportunity for higher management to get an in-depth and quick feel for the condition of the department. The facts, figures, and problems brought up in the planning meeting will bare the issues of the operation to the bone, but then the bone will flesh out again

with solutions and goals. Managers at any level can sit in on the meeting for 30 minutes and have enough information to get a picture of what is happening.

I have gone into the whys and hows of the planning process in depth because it represents the heart of basic management principles. Is it too basic to say that if you are going to achieve any goal you must plan first?

EXECUTING THE PLAN

We have located the work, counted, sorted, prioritized, and planned it. The question now becomes, how do we execute the plan? The alternatives are few. The employees may pick up the work and take it back to their desks, or the supervisor can walk the work to the employees.

If the supervisor has planned the day, the supervisor must personally execute the plan. The supervisor must choose who is to receive what work and hand it out. This provides the smooth and consistent flow. It also ensures reasonableness. The supervisor matches the work to the abilities of the employees. This is the time to recall my example of a 13-minute erosion in the daily efficiency of each employee on a 100-employee staff. (See example 2, page 40.) The supervisor needs a fine-tuning control to deal with such close tolerances. It takes an interpersonal relationship, with the supervisor personally executing the plan. The employees deserve to be assigned work that is accurately matched to their training and experience levels—their competency levels. People are individuals. Any management approach should give the supervisor the techniques to accommodate this reality.

Returning firstline supervision to management basics does have its problems. A certain number of supervisors do not want the interpersonal relationship that comes with active management. The truth is that they really do not want to get involved with their employees. Let's face it, though, management is founded on involvement.

115

I consider supervision as an active involvement with a unit's work and a unit's employees. What does the average supervisor consider supervision to be?

A Supervisor's View of Management

Based on a study I conducted in 1980, this is what the supervisors themselves feel supervision is all about.

1. Handling problem tasks. That is, personally handling the task, not supervising others in solving it.

2. Pitching in when work gets backed up.

3. Carrying out performance evaluations, salary administration, and general personnel functions.

4. Conducting training.

5. Observing desk tops and bins to see if work is backing up.

As you can imagine, the list goes tediously on.

I found it very interesting that the vast majority, if not all of the items on the list, could be done at the supervisor's desk. The real security blanket was: (1) Handling problem tasks. Experience tells me that most firstline supervisors are promoted almost solely on the basis of technical skill. If you weren't sure about how to supervise, but had a thorough understanding of a technical skill, to what would you gravitate?

The Need for Supervisors' Involvement

Let's return to the subject of this section, execution. My rule is that the supervisor must quantify the work for each employee and hand it to that employee at least twice a day. The amount of work handed out should occupy the employee for at least one hour but not more than four.

If we can get the supervisor accustomed to this personal approach by insisting the supervisor do it just twice a day, the supervisor will recognize active work assignment as a significant supervisory tool. When that occurs, this procedure will become a natural and flexible personal tool and not an artifically imposed rule handed down from top management. And this is exactly what happens. A routine develops. Work is handed out once in the morning and twice in the afternoon or twice both in the morning and in the afternoon.

A problem can arise, however. The essence of this procedure is to have the work *thought out*, not handed out. Handing the work out is only the execution of the thought process (planning). Please note the subtle implication of the last two sentences. To manage properly, the supervisor must think. Many present-day efficiency systems are structured around robotlike execution.

The problem is that some experienced supervisors tend to revert to their personal version of management . . . to their old supervisory ways. This makes for a very real problem. Now the supervisor is starting to do two jobs: to perform the new supervisory role and to continue to carry the unit by personally handling all its problems. What slips first is the planned thought process. At 1 p.m. the supervisor grabs a stack of work and hands it to an employee without thinking about what is in that stack of work. It may represent two hours of work, it may represent five. It may have work in it that the employee can't handle. All we know is that the supervisor distributed a stack of work and that the poor employee is stuck at his or her desk until 4:30 with either too much or too little work. *Again we can see that when management drops the ball, it falls first on the individual employee.*

We remedy this problem by installing a supervisory control to ensure that the supervisor exercises proper thought processes. The employee can go home after finishing the last assignment of the day. No questions asked. If the supervisor does not think the assignment through, employees could be getting up and leaving an hour or more early even though the department has work to do. Also, the supervisor does not have the recourse of overdistributing the work. All work left unfinished at the end of the day must go back into the work area to be recounted, sorted, prioritized, and planned. In other words, the supervisor would only be adding to her or his own workload. I call letting an employee go home early with pay an "early out." (I discuss this procedure more thoroughly in the next chapter.)

This touches on a subject that deserves more elaboration. A major problem we run into is the resistance of a supervisor to relinquishing old supervisory habits and accepting a totally new system of supervision. Supervisors, on the whole, are willing to embrace the new system; that is not the problem. The problem is getting supervisors to give up their old duties. As I pointed out, what actually happens is that they try to do both. That drives them right up the wall, and then a series of compromises begins. The result is always at the expense of the new duties.

The solution to this problem and numerous other problems that are inherent in such a sweeping change of systems centers around the techniques, competency, and experience of the individuals installing the program. The success of any new management approach will not be better than the quality of the managers who receive it. Also, the approach will not rise above the level of the competency of the individuals installing it. In this case, expert outside help will pay for itself several times over. As we shall see shortly, it could easily be the difference between success and failure.

8

The Answer

If you have followed everything in the text until now, and assuming that you are not way ahead of me, you should be waiting for the second shoe to drop.

Remember my earlier analogy to vodka. When white collar waste is locked-up potential, it cannot be seen, tasted, or smelled. It is intangible. Our chore is to turn this waste into something tangible so it can be dealt with and managed.

It is now obvious what productivity improvement course I suggest to bring about productivity savings in either a unit or an entire company. That was the purpose of discussing the 4/8 Theory, basic management approaches, and measurement. The second shoe deals with ways to capture productivity savings.

If everything I've said so far about the 4/8 Theory and the benefits of a smooth and consistent workflow is true, then as soon as we install a back-to-management-basics productivity improvement system, excess labor capacity must become apparent immediately. After all, haven't I been saying that, in a hypothetical unit of 10 people, the installation of an effective productivity improvement system is tantamount, on the first day, to having 11 to 15 employees show up to perform the work of 10?

That is exactly what happens. Whether it is 11 or 15 equivalent employees depends on the caliber of the management in question. The system will deliver the potential of 15 (6/8). In any event, the average unit will demonstrate that it is overstaffed from day one of the installation of the procedures. As stated earlier, the exception is the unit with a large backlog. In that case, the system manifests its potential by immediately commencing to get rid of the backlog.

In hundreds of installations, I have only been disappointed four or five times with nondramatic results. The disappointments came in units with severe backlogs and an inexperienced work force. In that case, no matter what approach you take, you are in for a prolonged period of rolled-up sleeves and perspiration. Thankfully, that is the exception.

The general rule is that the system runs the unit out of work. This fact is demonstrated by having a large portion of the work force run out of work at various hours during the day. Proper planning will enable you to predict this phenomenon in the morning meeting, right down to the individual and the hour. As soon as excess capacity is exhibited (made tangible), it must be dealt with. If the developed excess labor capacity cannot be absorbed by handling increased production, it still must be dealt with. This is important because an installation is usually not timed to a growth cycle.

The Cardinal Rule of Productivity Improvement

Remove excess employees from the unit's normal workflow as soon as you identify them.

I'm assuming that you cannot deal with the issue through increased output; therefore, you must deal with it through controlled input.

As a result of an organized return to basic management principles, management has a visual and, therefore, tangible control over the excess labor capacity in its operation. Up till now, unwittingly, the individual employees have been the repository of that control.

Once you have control of the excess labor capacity in your operation, you must act swiftly and decisively to consolidate and maintain that control. If you do not act swiftly and decisively, the operation in question will gradually manipulate the new productivity improvement system and recover and reabsorb the excess labor capacity. In a normal installation, the difference between a 10-percent productivity gain and a 50-percent productivity gain is the company's success in controlling the excess labor capacity that has been developed. This is where management caliber demonstrates itself.

As part of my productivity improvement approach, I use a procedure called reserve hours. As soon as an employee runs out of work, that employee must be taken out of the unit's normal workflow. The hours thus captured are referred to as reserve hours. Once you have excess capacity in a manageable form, you must preserve it. *It is almost a law of nature, an axiom, that unattended excess labor capacity returns to an intangible, unmanageable state.*

There are a number of ways you can deal with the issue of excess labor capacity besides by accommodating growth:

1. Doing additional training/cross-training.

2. Completing special projects.

3. Shifting employees to other units.

4. Sending employees home with pay.

5. Sending employees home without pay.

6. Terminating employees.

In order of priority, I advise 1, 2, 3, and 4. When your recovered excess capacity is large, you have to employ all four alternatives. Rather quickly, alternatives 1 and 2 come to an end, and you are left depending on 3 and 4.

Alternatives 5 and 6 are swift and efficient but not generally accepted in white collar industries. I have found that a hiring freeze (natural attrition) will bring a unit to the proper staffing level within three to nine months without the trauma, ill feelings, and morale issues associated with the more drastic alternatives.

In the mid-1960's, I was involved in installing an efficiency system in a very large foreign lumber mill. The mill was unionized. The union was friendly and enlightened and agreeable to increased efficiency, as long as it did not involve work speedup or layoffs. As I said, the mill was large; it took our team of nine consultants close to a year to complete the project. During that year, no voluntarily terminating employees were replaced. By the end of the year, the mill was running quite nicely with 20-percent fewer employees. I admit that natural attrition is a more realistic approach in the white collar area than in blue collar industries. And certainly more realistic in good times than in a recession. Natural attrition is a real solution, however, and therefore should be considered as an alternative to layoffs. Also, because increased efficiency can lead to excess labor, you do not have the alternative to ignore it.

Another consideration in favor of natural attrition is that it is unlikely you can install a system all at once throughout an entire company, even a small company. You will get far better cooperation and far better results if your purpose is not confused with laying off people.

That is not your purpose?

Does that surprise you?

The Purpose of a Productivity Enhancement Program

Your purpose is to place the company in a position to deal intelligently with the issue of staffing. For the first 6 to 12 months, the productivity improvement program will probably deal with overstaffing. By the end of that 6- to 12-month period, the unit's staffing should be in line. From then on, for all the decades of the future, the productivity program should focus primarily on proper, *increased staffing.*

There are two basic approaches under which you take an employee out of the unit's normal workflow. The following is a description of each of these approaches and the rationale for them.

When Should an Employee Leave the Workflow?

1. Reserve Hours

This refers to planned reassignment. An employee is taken out of the unit's normal workflow before the end of the day for special training or projects; to work in another unit; or, as a last resort, to go home with pay.

Identifying reserve hours in the planning meeting is a productivity improvement technique. This is the plug that, when pulled, allows excess capacity to become visible and therefore manageable. As excess employee time becomes available, it is identified and placed in reserve. You must then immediately deal with the reserve status. When you think of reserve hours using this "plug" analogy, you can more readily understand the need to maintain a reserve-hour policy in perpetuity.

Remember, work flows through any office in a cycle. If you are properly staffed, you should have reserve hours available during the daily, weekly, and monthly low points of the cycle. The number of reserve hours available indicates whether you are properly staffed or overstaffed. An absence of reserve hours signals understaffing not, as you might assume, proper staffing.

A strange phenomenon occurs regarding reserve hours. Both supervisors and managers want the reserve-hour accumulations to stop and stop soon. Both groups want to improve productivity, but they find the immediate results of this approach embarrassing. They can live with an excess person here or there spread out over 6 to 12 months, but watching bunches of excess employees develop over the period of a few days drives them up a wall. So many excess people suddenly appear that sending the employees home with pay is a daily reality. There is simply not enough work left to keep the entire staff occupied.

Some supervisors immediately start fictional training programs to keep people busy. Others transfer people indiscriminately to understaffed areas primarily to get them out of sight, secondarily to help out. In the latter example, top-level technical employees inundate someone's file department where there is a backlog. The results are that the technical employees are angry about having to peform work below their ability and the file department can't handle all the extra people. At least they are out of sight, though. Training and transferring people can be very constructive. The approach just described, however, is a common reaction that is not constructive.

Vice presidents have asked me, "When is this reserve-hour thing over with?" "What is my proper staffing so I can stop sending people home?" The well-informed attitude would be, "As long as I am accumulating reserve hours, I'm increasing my productivity and decreasing my expenses. I would hate to see the reserve hours diminish." There is always the underlying worry that sending people home with pay will be so attractive that natural attrition will cease. That does not happen. People always manage to rotate out.

Identifying reserve hours is the way we pull the plug on pent-up productivity potential. If you stop this procedure, you put back the plug. In that case, I guarantee your operation will again become bloated with people.

You might ask, "Can I eliminate this excess capacity by terminating employees?" The answer is "Yes," but realistically you will have to accumulate reserve hours for some time to get an idea of how many hours you can eliminate. Even after the terminations, however, you will have to use the reserve-hour method or you will plug up your operation and it will become overstaffed again.

2. Early Outs.

This refers to allowing employees to go home early with pay because of *misplanning*. (Reserve hours involve the *planned* release of employees.)

The last assignment for the day is accompanied by a green assignment ticket that signifies, "Go home when you are through with this." This is both a teaching tool *for* the supervisor and a management monitoring tool *of* the supervisor. It is not a reward for the employee. We do our best to avoid early outs through good planning.

The supervisor should plan the workday for the unit and then make the plan happen. It is apparent, therefore, that the supervisor must plan accurately. What better way to be sure both that the supervisor is planning and that the plan is accurate than to let the employees go home early when the supervisor plans poorly. This is a simple, visible tool. For the supervisor it is a learning tool, and for management it is a control tool; for the employee it should be a rare experience.

When they first use this tool, supervisors and managers have a problem with it. The supervisors feel it is a control over their activities. *Let's face it, in white collar industries most supervisors are not monitored.* Managers get fidgety about the tool because they see employees going home early with pay while there is still work to be done. To cope with the hesitant supervisor and the fidgety manager, stick with the tool. As is the case with most teaching/control tools, it will provide its own solution. The supervisor learns to plan and execute the program accurately. When that occurs, the early outs quickly become few and far between. Yet, they can become both frequent and significant if supervisory accuracy and execution become sloppy.

Also consider this aspect of the green ticket early out. If you did not use this tool, would employees handle more work because of the time available when they run out of work early? No. In that case, they will not let themselves run out.

Where does that leave you? You are not sure. And, that is the situation that all this is trying to prevent or correct.

The green ticket and the attending early out is a supervisory control technique. Sending employees home because of lack of work as a result of the planning meeting is a productivity improvement technique. Please note the difference. Managers should use reserve hours and early outs. They should be jealous of any erosion of either concept, because what is being eroded is control over staffing and, therefore, control over productivity.

Remember this simple point: when it comes to these concepts, productivity and corporate expenses are the issue. Today, backlog manages white collar America. If you are a manager, it is up to you to decide whether backlog will continue to run your unit or whether *you* are going to run the unit. The issue is not the ability of the supervisor to run the unit without reserve hours or early outs. They don't need them, you do.

9

A Case Study

A case study is an excellent tool with which to pull together the theory and logic outlined in earlier chapters. Up till now we have been discussing the issue of white collar productivity on an academic plane. An actual back-to-management-basics case study will tie together the procedural and substantive methodologies. You must pay careful, sensitive attention to analyzing and installing a productivity management program. A client company, or a client unit within a company, has the right to be approached with the same thoughtful skill that was invested in developing the program that will be brought to them.

The case study illustrates that no program installation methodology is perfect. Yet, you can substantially reduce the trauma of change. In any corporate reorganization of a unit, you should involve the unit in the conceptual stage as well as in the installation stage. And I do not mean in a passive role. I have yet to have a client unit disagree with this. Changing the working way of life of individuals is a personal encounter. Such a change should be orchestrated within the immediate corporate family. As will be pointed out in chapter 11, the client should be trained to perform all the installation duties associated with the eventual changes in its operating method. The first step is for the outside consultant to organize, and then to train, the corporate productivity department.

But, even in a modest-sized company, is the corporate productivity department a part of the immediate "field" family? No! It is home office! When the corporate productivity department brings change to the field, it must in turn involve the field. It must involve the field in the development of the change as well as in the installation of the change. As it turns out, the corporate productivity department assumes the role of inside consultant. When the corporate productivity department goes into the field, it does so as an orchestra conductor. The conductor may take several lead players along from home office, but the orchestra of installers is drawn from the field. This means that before every performance, the productivity department spends a considerable amount of time training field help. In this case, "field" can represent an actual field office or any unit whose supervisory style is to be reorganized. There are three roles to be played in an installation:

1. The corporate role is that of advisor and trainer.

2. The project leader or leaders are supervisors from the field functional area in question, but not the unit in question, who are trained to lead the installation.

3. The installation team is a group of supervisors drawn together from other units to help the project leaders. The size of the installation team depends on the size of the office where the program is to be installed. It is your task to go into the department and change its method of managing. You will also change the basic workflow of the entire department. You have a big task ahead of you. Consequently, you cannot skimp on help. You will need one installation team member for each supervisor. You also need the encouragement and understanding gained by involving individuals who are driven by the compassion that comes from kindred spirits.

Kindred Spirits

The concept of kindred spirits is of particular value when working with the "knowledge worker." We recently dealt with a 1,200-employee claim department made up of 29 claim offices. Seventy percent of that work force was made up of knowledge workers. The educational level of this group ran the gamut from the "school of hard knocks" to law degrees. All these employees spent a major portion of their workday in think time.

We brought claim management into the conceptualizing process of the back-to-management-basics changes as they applied to their function. The result was that:

1. We were confident that we were not interfering with the technical process because the technical experts helped us.

2. The technical experts had confidence in us, because they had input.

3. The managers of the knowledge workers had an ownership interest in the project.

To bring the project closer to the supervisors, who were the primary object of the program, we dealt exclusively with them in the activity- and workflow-analysis phase. Once that phase was completed, we gave classroom and on-the-job training to a select group of these supervisors in how to install the new procedures. We used eight office installations as on-the-job-training for the new project leaders. They then took over from the corporate productivity department as the project leaders for the remaining claim offices.

You can't solve the "outsider" issue simply by involving the field personnel in an installation leadership role. Remember my comment that change should be orchestrated within the immediate corporate family. This is where the installation team builds on the immediate corporate family concept. Given the task of installing the program in claim office A, which has six supervisors, the new project leader calls for six supervisors (installation team) to be loaned for three or four weeks from offices B, C, D, etc. The project leader, with the help of the corporate productivity department, trains the installation team. The installation team then goes to office A and performs the installation, knowing full well their office may be next and that a supervisor from A will be there to help them.

By the time the process gets to office M, an enormous amount of experienced field help is available. By then, one of your major problems will be to control the premature installation fever that will be springing up in the remaining units. Once you get a "roll" such as this started, your biggest problem is no longer acceptance but is instead overeagerness.

Selecting the First Site

We have discussed why the installers are chosen. How is the first site picked? The first site, or the initial several sites, are very important. You must plan the first installation in a positive and receptive atmosphere. This gives you the opportunity to test the new concepts you've developed and set the tone for future installations. By correctly choosing a prime location for your first installation, you can maximize the overall success of your program. It is important to gain control of the field grapevine immediately with a potent success story.

Establishing a Work Plan and Gathering Data

The corporate productivity department and the field project leader perform the first-phase work. The installation team is used primarily during the actual installation.

In the first phase of the project, a work plan is put together. This includes a detailed timetable for the project, individual responsibilities, and expected results of each activity. After the work plan is completed, attention is turned to data-gathering. This is done at a cross section of sites, or at the site in question if only one is involved. At this point, individual workers and their supervisors explain how their operation works or why it doesn't work and suggest improvements. They do this through individual employee sessions and group supervisor sessions. *I cannot overemphasize the enormous information reservoir that lies within this group.* They know where the office minefield is, but they can't defuse it. On the other hand, management can defuse the field but doesn't know where it is (or maybe even that it exists).

Preparing the Workflow

An equally important part of this phase is the sorting out of the workflow issues. The best way to approach this problem is through a group supervisory session. *Today, all across white collar America, groups of supervisors work as individuals. They must start working as a team.* The workflow analysis is a good starting place. This group self-examination shakes out many problems and is, therefore, a shortcut for the corporate productivity department in organizing the workflow. Needless to say, the final workflow is a result of the efforts and input of the supervisors. The corporate productivity department and the field project leader act as catalysts.

Workflow is nothing more than a stream of individual work activities flowing through an office. It is not enough to set the correct course for this flow; you must fully understand the individual activities. This leads us to the next phase: work-task analysis. The laborious part of this phase is the fine analysis of all individual work tasks that make up the unit's output. To plan work, you must measure the individual activities. This can be an emotional phase, because the employees and their supervisors may think you will use the information to increase rate. You can mitigate this issue through communications sessions that train and involve the supervisors in the measurement process. In other words, bring the measurement process down, as close as possible, to the basic corporate family unit. When you are dealing with a succession of similar operational units, you need complete this process only once. In the succeeding units, the analysis and measurement tasks will boil down to simply the issue of fine tuning and personalizing the process unit by unit.

If you follow the procedures I have described, no substantive surprises will await you. Earlier, I said you could mitigate the trauma of change. Why not eliminate it? Unfortunately, we cannot completely prepare for individual reactions to the actual stress of change. The installation will probably take several weeks; everything will not progress on cue. As you will see, we can prepare for the installation stress, but we cannot completely eliminate it.

Installing Workflow Changes

The actual installation of a project also breaks down into phases. First it will take one to two weeks to install the workflow corrections. The actual change in workflow takes one day. Since the supervisors heavily influenced the final workflow recommendations, a broad, intuitive preparation has already taken place. Under the leadership of the corporate productivity director and/or the field project leader, the supervisors and installation team members freeze all work in progress. Every piece of work is located, identified, evaluated, and integrated into the new workflow through revised routing slips. This process must take place in snapshot fashion. Needless to say, the period devoted to the freeze is intense and must be well-organized and planned. The one- to two-week time frame given to the entire workflow phase is to provide shakedown time.

For an explanation of the second intallation phase, let's take an actual case history of a processing department in an insurance company.

132

PREINSTALLATION ACTIVITIES

It was a Wednesday morning when the corporate project director and a corporate project consultant arrived at the office. They had arranged an afternoon meeting with corporate personnel and local management. After making sure everything was properly set up, they began the afternoon meeting at 1 o'clock.

In attendance were the executive vice president, divisional vice president, project leader (the field manager chosen to head the installation), and local office manager. The corporate representatives gave two slide presentations. The first one, presented by the corporate project director, covered the theory of the program, its logic, and its methodology. The corporate project consultant presented another group of slides covering installation considerations and completely reviewed the installation mechanics (including all forms used). Following the presentations, the people-side of the installation was discussed. It was pointed out that management and supervisory personnel make a substantial investment of time during an installation.

Two very interesting reactions from the group should be noted here. The office manager about to receive the installation indicated that the program would not have much impact since his office was "already using work management." (The interesting feature about this particular project is it was being put in an office where a work management/measurement system had been installed in the mid-seventies.)

A counterreaction came from the executive vice president. He saw through the statements made by the office manager and began asking questions about how management people could be held accountable for productivity results after an installation. He asked specifically if the office manager could and should be held accountable for the level of productivity attained (or not attained) in the office. He attempted to communicate to the office manager that the current issue was reduced expenses. This interchange had the intended impact on the office manager; his attention was piqued.

INSTALLATION TEAM TRAINING

The next day, Thursday, was designated as the day to begin the training of the field project leader and the installation team members in all facets of the program. The project leader had served on two prior installations. He was an installation team member and he was the office manager in an office that had received an installation. Since he had served on both sides of the installation fence, he had a good grasp of the program. His training amounted to little more than reviewing the forms and mechanics, after which he was ready to conduct the training of the installation team members.

The installation team members were all supervisors. Several had previous installation experience; only one had no previous exposure to the program. The installation team training started that Thursday at noon and lasted through Friday. Each installation team member was assigned to a supervisor in the office.

The corporate productivity personnel attended the training session and were available to help out if needed, but most of the training was done by the project leader. The project leader reviewed the question: Why is our productivity declining?; then, program logic, the 4/8 Theory, the 6/8 Theory, and the concept of excess capacity were developed and discussed by the group.

Next came a thorough review of the mechanics of the program. The project leader showed the installation team the different forms the supervisors would use. Various concepts were presented and discussed, such as work being "frozen" temporarily so that it could be quantified, and the project leader covered "work that comes in today is handled by employees tomorrow."

There was substantial discussion on plan execution. If there was one point that the project leader emphasized, it was that execution of the plan translates to direct supervision. The project leader also pushed the concept of supervisory followup. He pointed out that planning and execution are dependent on good followup to ensure that events happen as intended.

The next phase of the training took the installation team members through a series of exercises. This involved filling out all the program's control and planning forms. This exercise was meant to bring the concepts together and emphasize that though the elements themselves are simple to understand, keeping them all sorted out can be confusing. It gave the installation team some idea of the level of confusion supervisors might experience while learning how to complete the forms.

It is interesting to note just how confusing things got for the installation team. One team member calculated that 5.18 hours of work existed in the imaginary work unit. Another calculated 12.18 hours. Another calculated 18.6 hours! They identified and discussed all the reasons why they'd come up with various results.

The last item on the agenda was the presentation of the sensitivity training program. The team discussed the reasons for its use and how it would be presented to the supervisors.

The project leader pointed out that the next activity would be to get into the various work units and set up the supervisory work areas. This meant getting the various shelves in the storage cabinets labeled and ready to receive work. The group established a schedule and then adjourned.

THE INSTALLATION

Monday

The first objective Monday morning was to have the office manager conduct a tour of the office with the installation team. Since this team was drawn from other locations, it was important that the team members be able to relate their knowledge to the physical layout of this particular office. The tour started with observing the early morning mail routine and then proceeded from work station to work station observing how an insurance policy was processed. The mail routine started in the premium department; clerks opened the mail, processed checks and applications for insurance, and performed a cashiering function. The group then moved on to the underwriting department to observe how applications were handled. Here, underwriters reviewed newly submitted insurance risks for acceptability. The group observed a customer service unit, in which employees received incoming calls from insurance agents and policyholders. The next area in the tour was the data entry unit, in which all computer entry occurred. Then the group moved to the control/records unit. Here computer output was printed, burst, sorted, and matched to source documents. Lastly, the group viewed the final step in the production line, the microfilming process.

In the afternoon, supervisory training, conducted by the project leader, started with the theory, logic, and mechanics of the program. At the appointed time, the installation team, supervisors, and office manager, as well as the two corporate respresentatives, convened to begin training.

The project leader began by discussing declining unit productivity. What followed was an intense, in-depth training session. A great deal of attention was paid to the concept of reserve hours; these were portrayed as a demonstration of increasing productivity. The supervisors were shown how to put this captured excess capacity to work. The group then discussed when to send employees home with pay. The supervisors were told to do this when they had no reasonable alternatives (such as transferring employees to other units, conducting training programs, or getting employees involved in special projects).

Then came the sensitivity training program. Supervisors go through an attitude cycle during an installation. Their attitude starts high, drops, bottoms out, climbs, and ends on a high note. We recognized several years ago that this swing in supervisory attitude was consistent from one project to another. The attitude cycle was so consistent, in fact, that we were eventually able to predict to the exact day in an installation when supervisory attitudes would hit bottom.

Armed with this knowledge, we set out to try to minimize or, if possible, eliminate the downward shift in supervisory enthusiasm. We interviewed supervisors and managers in whose operations the program had been installed. We found that many times frustration surfaced as a result of fear or preconceived notions regarding the program and how it would personally affect supervisors and managers. Through interviews and analysis, we discovered four areas in which supervisors most often had concerns:

1. Supervisors' perception of themselves as being on trial.
2. The change in relationship perceived likely to occur between supervisor and employee because of assigning and physically distributing work to employees.
3. The perception that this program added more work to the already overloaded supervisor's workday.
4. The fear of reserve hours and early outs and how they would be interpreted by the supervisor's peers and top management.

At this point, we decided our installations would work much better by dealing with the emotional issues up front. Thus, we developed the sensitivity session.

This session is basically an exercise in group dynamics. The supervisors are split into two or more groups. Each group deals with one or more of the above issues, and one group deals with an all other category. Each group meets for a period of time to develop a list of reasons why their assigned issue could cause a supervisor concern. Then a spokesperson from each group lists each reason, and the project leader responds in front of the whole group.

Typical statements include:

"This program has been successful in other units. If it's unsuccessful in my unit, people will think it's my fault."

"I feel the reason you're here is because others think I haven't been doing a good job."

"If we run out of work and my employees have nothing to do, will my boss think I should have recognized I'm overstaffed?"

"What will be the reaction of my employees when I deliver their work to them?"

"With all the work I'm currently doing, how will I ever get time to do this? I'm already working overtime."

"How will my employees feel about going home early?"

We have found that supervisors and managers respond well to this sensitivity session. Additionally, we have learned where we were deficient in our initial communication sessions and have upgraded them to be sure that participants properly interpret what we say. This session had helped minimize the supervisor attitude cycle.

You must, however, do more than conduct this session in order to minimize the problem. In addition you must:

• Communicate clearly, concisely, and continually with managers, supervisors, and employees.

• Provide complete training programs for managers and supervisors.

• Fully train installation persons to provide one-on-one assistance to each supervisor.

• Have upper levels of management totally involved in the project.

• Conduct an informal event for supervisors away from the office when attitudes are at their lowest.

The last item is an important one. We can predict the attitude curve to the day. Upon initiating an installation, the project leader will request that management sponsor an informal gathering of all managers, supervisors, and installers. This will be scheduled for an evening close to the time the attitude cycle is at its low point. The gathering need be nothing more than a cookout or perhaps a pizza party.

There are attitude cycles in every installation. Their magnitude, however, varies. It has been our experience that, when worked out, the down cycle can be minimized to a point at which it is almost inconsequential.

Tuesday

Tuesday morning, the installation team members joined their supervisors in the work units. The supervisors started their employees on the work in the unit. Each supervisor and installation team member discussed how to keep the employees busy while bringing all remaining items of work into the supervisor's area. This involved the inspection of all work stations to make sure that nothing was left in the desks, on the desks, or in the storage cabinets next to the employees' work stations. The rest of the morning and through the early afternoon the team did just that. At about 3 p.m. the supervisor and installation team member set about developing their plan for Wednesday, which some teams did not complete until after 7 p.m.

Wednesday

The daily planning schedules were finished, assignments were ready for distribution, the planning worksheets were completed and turned in to the meeting leader. At 9 a.m., the first planning meeting began.

Usual attendance at a planning meeting is the office management and supervisory staff. During an installation, the meeting also includes the corporate representative, the project leader, and the installation team.

In the preinstallation communication session, the office manager was told that the program results would be dramatic, immediate, and tangible. These results were borne out in the first planning meeting. Even with 13 percent of the work force on vacation and 7 percent out sick, the attendees at the meeting were able to identify an additional 8 percent of the work force as reserve hours. Reserve time was primarily put to work by lending employees across unit lines. Some employees were sent home early with pay. Members of the management team expressed surprise; they had been convinced that they were running a tight office and that they were not overstaffed. After all, hadn't they been working with a formal work management/measurement system? They had felt that, if anything, they were perhaps a bit understaffed and were shocked at the dramatic and immediate identification of reserve hours.

139

As is always the case, the first planning meeting was a long one, lasting well over an hour.

The afternoon was committed to further organization of the supervisory work areas. It was a little hard for one supervisor to avoid the tendency to dip into tomorrow's work for assignments for her employees who were running out of work. To the credit of the office manager, the supervisor was counseled to resist the temptation to give the person something to do from tomorrow's plan.

An interesting situation arose in one of our earlier installations concerning the holding of today's incoming work for tomorrow. A unit decided not to hold work. You can guess what happened. The unit invented a new concept called late ins (as contrasted with early outs). Since the supervisors in the unit had not held any work, they had no work to give their employees the next day. They had to call the employees and tell them not to come in in the morning until they could organize that day's mail. Obviously they did not stick with this new concept very long. This shows how closely work can be planned. It has to be planned to very close tolerances if you are going to recognize 13 minutes of time erosion in an employee's day.

As the afternoon wore on and the quantification of the work continued, a few disturbing things began to happen. Much to the surprise of the supervisors, people who had received their last assignment were beginning to leave the office early. This was the first proof to the supervisors that they needed to modify their plans.

Problems developed in the premium unit, which was using historical data as the basis for the next day's plan. All units handle cash work on a same-day basis. The plan did not come off as intended, because far more mail was received than was normally the case. On this particular day, the premium unit received nearly 900 checks for processing instead of the usual 500. In the midst of these developments, the premium unit still quantified the work for the next day and finalized plans for Thursday. The supervisors and the installation team left the office that night about 6:30.

Thursday

At the morning planning meeting, the management team discussed the fact that, at various times during the day, 60 percent of the people in the office would run out of work. The total reserve hours were equivalent to about 23 percent of the full-time employees, even with vacation absences running at 13 percent and sick time at 7 percent of the work force.

The supervisory group struggled with what to do with all the reserve hours. Projects began to spring up everywhere. The office manager resisted most of these temptations to bottle up the excess time. In fact, he encouraged his people to send the nonsupervisory employees home with pay if they had nothing to do. He acknowledged the overstaffing for that day and emphasized to the supervisors that things could and perhaps would be different the next day.

During the meeting, one of the installation team members observed, regarding reserve hours, vacation, and people out sick, "Wow, that's nearly half the office staff identified as either unavailable or unneeded, and the office can still maintain currency. What a statement about staffing!"

Next, the premium unit supervisor lodged a strong complaint about "in today, out tomorrow." "It's not working!" she complained, "My plan is not based on reality!" The project leader counseled her to "stay with it" to get more experience. "It will work out," he assured her. On that note, the planning meeting ended.

The supervisors spent the balance of the morning executing the plan. Quantification of Friday's work began Thursday afternoon. By late Thursday afternoon, morale was beginning to slide. People with green assignment tickets were leaving early. By 5 p.m. the plans were not shaping up well for Friday. The supervisors were complaining about "Rules! Rules! Rules!" It seemed as though the system was running the office. The premium unit supervisor by this time was fit to be tied. The afternoon plan was not making sense. Nothing was working out as planned.

141

By 6:30 that evening, the last supervisor left the office expressing a high degree of frustration.

Friday

The project leader was nervous when he came to work Friday morning. It was obvious that he had spent a lot of time during the night thinking about the problems in the premium unit. He was worried about the daily cash deposit. He was worried about the morale of the supervisor as well as the office manager. For the premium unit, the plan for Friday was similar to other plans that week—tentative. It was based on historical data, not real work. That bothered him. The project leader understood that it was necessary to get your arms around all the work at one time. He felt this approach was not working in the premium unit due to the problems developing from estimated work volumes.

The project leader developed an alternative approach. Tentative assignments for employees would be written today for tomorrow based on historical data, with a plan to open the mail and count all the work each morning to develop specific assignments based on actual receipts, not projections. At the Friday morning planning meeting the project leader described his change in approach to the premium department. The new approach seemed to please the office manager and the premium unit supervisor. There was no change in the in today-out tomorrow concept for the other units in the office.

At the Friday planning meeting, participants discussed the staffing situation and how the office would maintain currency with people out sick and on vacation while generating reserve hours.

Supervisors expressed some concerns over employees leaving the office early with pay. This didn't seem equitable to two of the supervisors who were worried about possible employee reactions. The project leader took the correct stand. He told them to continue to send employees home early whenever they could not use reserve hours. The intangibleness of white collar efficiency was becoming tangible and thus manageable. It had to remain that way.

The group also discussed the need for the Monday plans to include some thoughts on how the Monday mail opening would be handled. The Monday morning mail, in that office, represented about three to four times the normal mail volume handled daily on Tuesday through Friday. The supervisors agreed to allocate more people to the opening of the mail on a controlled, planned basis. The office manager brought reports to the meeting that indicated that, with the additional people, it would take about half an hour to get the mail opened. The supervisors committed to provide help in opening the mail.

The group also talked about service. While members of the group identified no particular service problems, they agreed that service should continue to be a prominent part of the regular agenda for each day's planning meeting. They had discussed service and quality as part of the training preparation. The project leader pointed out that a formal approach to organization and planning enhances both issues.

This would seem to be an appropriate point at which to review the effect on service this installation had on this office. The corporate service standard was as follows: 90 percent of all work must be processed and issued within 10 working days from the date it is initially received in the office. This operation chose to increase that standard to 93 percent in 10 days.

Actual service for the four weeks before the installation was as follows:

Weeks	Standard 90 Percent In 10 Days
Fourth	96.0%
Third	92.0%
Second	95.5%
First	95.5%

During and after the two-week installation, service results were as follows:

Weeks	Standard 90 Percent In 10 Days
First week of installation	97%
Second week of installation	96%
First week after installation	97%

The office consistently processed all routine business in three to four working days. Only material that was received with missing information strained the service tolerances.

After the planning meeting, the supervisors returned to their work stations to "make Friday happen." Things seemed to be going pretty well through the morning. At noon things soured. The supervisor in charge of the premium unit became frustrated again and went home. The office manager took over the premium unit supervisory responsibilities for the afternoon. In addition, the office manager decided to move one of the nonsupervisory employees from underwriting into the premium unit to assist in building the plan for Monday.

One of the things that became obvious at this point was that the system had seemed to take over the management of the office. Everybody was hung up on rules: rules relative to assignments, the mechanics of followup, the mechanics of filling out the forms (do you multiply or divide by the planning factor?), and so on. This contributed to the supervisors' sense of frustration, a feeling of not really being in control. What they did not realize was that they were building the skills that would give them better control than they ever imagined they could have. But when it's late in the afternoon and things aren't going well, it's hard to see that reality.

By Friday afternoon spirits were low. It had been a long, difficult, frustrating week. One of the supervisors left after her husband had called about 6 p.m. wondering where she was. This was the third day in a row that she had not been home for dinner.

And so that week ended.

Monday, Second Week

Things looked much brighter Monday morning.

The supervisor of the premium department, who left Friday afternoon, was back Monday morning with a smile on her face.

The plan to bring more people into the premium department to open the mail was working. By 8:30 in the morning, the gang approach got the mail opened early.

Things were looking good!

In the morning planning meeting, the team discovered for the first time that, due to the heavy mail volume, the volume of work in the office exceeded the available employee time. While everyone was relieved at not having to cope with reserve hours that day, the team discussed a new problem: how to get current again.

The next agenda item at the meeting was a discussion of the numbers reflected on the planning summary form. Now the supervisors and managers were beginning to understand what the numbers were saying. But they were struggling with the procedure for documenting employees being shifted from a unit with reserve hours to a unit with a backlog. As they discussed these concepts, decisions were reached as to how everyone would uniformly document the transfer of hours of employee time. While the debate became very complex and heated at times, it was based on knowledge of the system by a group of people who were essentially trying to make the system more efficient.

Problems in the premium unit developed later that day. Just before lunch, the supervisor and the office manager sat down to discuss the situation. The supervisor said she didn't want to be a supervisor any more. The office manager and the supervisor then met with the project leader. The three of them concluded that the supervisor should give it another try.

As it turned out, Monday did run very smoothly for the premium unit, even with all the problems at the supervisory level. The unit executed the plan for the day, which was a good plan based on real numbers, along the lines originally developed. It was a successful day from the standpoint of plan execution.

While the plans for Tuesday developed very well in some units, a problem developed in the unit whose supervisor had not been home on time for several days. Just about the time that the plan for the day was to be wrapped up, the supervisor's husband called in again. The supervisor went home without completing her plan. This was unfortunate for another reason. This was the evening that the supervisors, installation team, and project leader met for a pizza party.

Tuesday, Second Week

It looked like a good day shaping up! The supervisor who went home at 6:00 the evening before was back at work. She promptly sat down and finished up the plan for the day. The day unfolded in the premium department without a hitch. Things looked good in that unit.

The daily planning meeting came off in routine fashion. It lasted about 15 minutes. No one had questions about procedures or how to handle the forms. It was obvious that the management team had overcome the problem of the system running the office. Now the managers were talking about the facts revealed on the planning sheets. It was obvious that they were in full command of the activities in their departments. The management team was back in control of the office!

This day seemed to be the turning point in the installation. The afternoon came off smoothly. All supervisors were out of the office and on their way home at 4:30 in the afternoon. Another accomplishment of the day was that everyone in the premium department was happy, including the supervisor.

All in all, Tuesday was administered by the management team with no disruption and no emotionalism. The plan for Wednesday looked good at the conclusion of the day.

146

Wednesday through Friday, Second Week

It became obvious on Wednesday that the installation team would soon no longer be needed.

Plans for the day were completed Wednesday morning. Individual employee assignments were distributed as planned, and the morning planning meeting came off without a hitch. While some questions and need for help always comes up at this point in an installation, the installation team found itself basically standing by.

The office manager and the supervisors began to make comments to the installation team reflecting their surprise at the staffing results. They expressed their satisfaction that the team had installed the program properly and that the employees had accepted it well.

The installation team left for home. Now it was up to the corporate project director, along with the local project leader to submit the wrap-up report to the executive vice president and to the divisional vice president.

The report was delivered to the top management people at 5 p.m. Friday. The report indicated that the mechanics of the program were in place in all the departments. The concepts, forms, controls, and other features of the program that had been introduced by the installation team were in place. The daily planning meeting was effective and it was following the prescribed format.

The corporate project director brought up the point that productivity had not been increased. This created a flurry of reaction from top management people who did not seem to understand that, while available work capacity had been demonstrated, productivity had not been affected. The corporate project director handled this part of the discussion. The point was made to the division vice president that, until staffing is reduced, as policy counts remain stable, or until the policy count goes up substantially with no change in staffing, productivity will not change. The distinction was clearly made between increasing a unit's capacity for work and improving a unit's level of productivity.

147

The executive vice president quickly resolved that issue. He had been disturbed for several months by a problem office in another city. He ordered that that office be closed and that all the work be transferred to this unit with no additional staffing. This took place, with considerable labor and overhead savings, both of which were documented in the macromeasurement report.

The project was treated well by the office grapevine. All during the installation, calls from other offices were pouring into this office. The office manager's reports were positive and exciting. This case study is not unusual, and yet no case study is absolutely representative. Each installation is unique.

10

Personal Productivity

The basic rules that apply to corporate productivity also apply to individual or personal productivity. In other words, personal productivity is amenable to analysis, planning, and execution. Most of you will take this opening statement for granted. It is simple and straightforward, one of those "who cares" statements.

What makes the statement true? That statement is true because personal productivity enhancement is no different from group productivity enhancement in that it has nothing to do with working harder or faster. There is no greater dampener to personal productivity than the feeling that the only alternative to our present lack of personal productivity is to get in there and work harder and faster.

Working Harder/Faster

Simply to work faster is to increase the risk of error. *Quality is developed through a consistent mode of work over time that in turn leads to experience.* Productivity and quality go hand-in-hand as an expression of experience. To request faster work is to request a change in the mode of work. The result will be a decline in quality that will more than offset the advantages of any increase in production. *Productivity and quality are so interdependent that one is implicit in the other.*

Another obvious issue is that the very term "speed up" indicates an unnatural mode of operation. We all understand that an unnatural mode of operation is not sustainable and therefore is not a durable solution. *Working faster is not a solution to white collar waste. It is not morally right, it is not durable, and it leads to counterproductive quality problems.*

Let me remind you again what the back-to-management-basics issue is. It simply means providing the methodology for individuals working at their normal speed to work more consistently through good management techniques. That applies in the aggregate to corporations and to all of us as individuals.

You will hear the harder/faster remarks from either the uninitiated or the detractor. The uninitiated soon become initiated, and the issue goes away. For the detractor, it is an insidious cheap shot. The terms "harder/faster," when related to productivity, hold an inherently superficial logic.

As noted, the description of a personal productivity improvement method illustrates the point that improved productivity is the result of the logical use of tested management principles. If you conduct yourself in an orderly, thoughtful fashion, you will be productive.

What does the 4/8 Theory mean to each of us? The 4/8 Theory generally holds true for all professions, all individuals. The executive who works a 10-hour day would be hard pressed to quantify 5 productive hours out of that day. This is true of the average salesperson just as it is of the average homemaker. It is true of everybody. The productivity reality is that in each one of us there is an additional half person as trained and as experienced as you and I. Let's break down the individual's productivity approach into the same basic parts we used in discussing the general productivity approach for corporations.

MACROMEASUREMENT

Macromeasurement is possible for the individual whose work tasks are repetitive. It does not take a great deal of time or an excessive amount of thought. What it does take is personal discipline. In the corporation, management/supervision supplies the disciplined methodolgy. For the individual, discipline is a personal thing. Personal discipline is the key to improving personal productivity and gaining its rewards.

If you are serious about improving your personal productivity, you must go through the same mental gymnastics as a corporation. As an example, how productive are you? Let's face it; even though you are you (a very personal relationship), you do not know the answer to that question.

To measure your personal productivity, you must determine your output; you must recognize your level of input. By dividing your input into your output, you should learn how efficient you are at whatever task you are measuring. As with the corporation, even with that effort, you do not know whether you are productive.

You will have to formulate a benchmark from which to measure progress. You will assume that you are not as productive as you would like to be and, therefore, progress becomes your motivation. Let's illustrate this by taking two totally different professions as our example. Let's use an insurance salesperson and a homemaker.

To establish a personal measuring device, all you need are a piece of paper and a pencil. List down the left side of the paper all the basic activities that represent output.

For an insurance salesperson, this could be the sale of (1) auto policies (2) homeowner policies (3) life policies, etc. It would not be prospecting, report writing, etc. Remember this is a macromeasurement system, not a daily plan.

For the homemaker, it could be (1) the dinner process, (2) grocery shopping, (3) cleaning house, etc. The list for the homemaker will be longer and more thought-provoking.

Planning as the Utilization of Time

Once the list is completed, you must analyze the list and determine which item takes the least amount of effort, measured in time, to complete. Remember, we are talking about time, not interest or intensity. Once you have picked the task that consumes the least amount of time, give it a factor of one. Then start at the top of your list and evaluate how much time each task takes as related to the base task with the factor of one. In this evaluation, exactness is not necessary; however, one should be ballpark close. Consistency will be the equalizer.

The key to a personal macromeasurement system is in the commonality of time. It should be noted that we never compare complexity of task. We do not compare creativity, performance, or intensity of the work to be measured. Increased personal or employee productivity is based on enhanced utilization of time. Let's compare two very different tasks. As an example, let's take a ditch digger and a nuclear physicist. The ditch digger has a hole to dig that will take 30 minutes. The physicist has a formula to solve that will also take 30 minutes. What is the only thing common between the two tasks? Thirty minutes.

Now, let's say that the physicist at home is a gardener, therefore, an occasional ditch digger. Let's then suppose that the physicist is at home on a Sunday with only two tasks that must be done that day: (1) solve a formula that will take 30 minutes and (2) dig a hole that will take 30 minutes. He has the whole day at his disposal, so neither job has priority. When the physicist sets out to plan these two activities, aside from preference, what is his only consideration? That there are two 30-minute time slots to fill. Nothing else matters for the simple act of measurement and planning.

The insurance salesperson could have a list that looks like the following:

Task	Factor
Homeowner sale	1.5
Auto sale	1.0
Small business policy	6.0
Individual life policy	3.5

The homemaker could have a list that looks like this:

Task	Factor
Completed dinner process	4.0
Completed lunch process	1.0
House cleaning	10.0
Grocery shopping	5.0

No two persons' lists will be the same. Why? Because we are talking about your own personal ability, which is accepted on its own merits. Activities, interests, and priorities vary from individual to individual. But there will always be a common thread linking all these personal productivity programs: all are based on the principles and techniques of effective time management.

Developing a Personal Productivity Measurement System

Once you have your list made, all you need to do is record how many times a day, week, or month you do each task. The following examples illustrate how our insurance salesperson goes about developing a personal productivity program:

Task	Factor		Times Completed Per Month		Accumulated Effort In Units
Homeowner Sale	1.5	×	4	=	6.0
Auto Sale	1.0	×	10	=	10.0
Small Business Sale	6.0	×	2	=	12.0
Individual Life Sale	3.5	×	5	=	17.5
TOTAL					45.5

The salesperson can now quantify the output, or numerator, because it has been reduced to common units. The apples and oranges issue is resolved. *A nuclear formula can be compared to a freshly dug hole, and what we find is that, as far as elapsed time is concerned, they are the same.*

Now you need a record of days or hours worked. This will be your denominator. Say the salesperson worked 240 hours that particular month. The salesperson's productivity for the month is 45.5 ÷ 240, or 1 ÷ 5.27, or about 5.27 hours of labor to produce a unit of work.

Is that good? No one knows. Aggressive salespersons however, will decide to consider themselves unproductive and will work at becoming more productive. Salespersons have to evaluate for themselves what the appropriate measuring period is: monthly, quarterly, biannually, annually. The first such period measured becomes the base period or the benchmark from which all progress will be measured.

As an example, 1 ÷ 5.27 reduces itself to a base factor of .189. Let's say that the next month the salesperson sells 47.5 units in 235 hours, or 47.5 ÷ 235, or 1 ÷ 4.94, which is a factor of .202. The salespersons's productivity is increased from .189 to .202, or .202 ÷ .189, or a productivity change-ratio 1.068, which indicates a 6.8-percent productivity increase. Always divide the current month's productivity factor by the base-period factor.

Now you have your personal macromeasurement system. Now you know where you are and you have the ability to measure your progress. But progress does not come without effort. Progress must be planned.

PLANNING

The next issue you have to decide is: What are you expecting from your increased productivity? For example, there is no point in developing a personal system that's passive. If you want increased productivity, grab the initiative and force the results you want. Make your day happen. Salespersons want increased income, increased sales volume. They should have a relatively good idea of how many prospective customers they need to generate a proposal of sale for each line of insurance. They should also know how many proposals have to be made to produce one completed sale. They know how much time, on an average, goes into prospecting and how much time is usually needed to develop and submit a proposal. With that information for each day, week, or month, they can back into the effort needed to accomplish the goal that has been set.

Developing a Personal Plan

As an example, say the salesperson sets a personal sales goal for a certain insurance line at $8,000 in premium. The average premium per sale is $2,000. Ergo four sales are needed. Let's assume further that this particular salesperson is hitting (making a sale) on every three sales proposals presented and, on average, must contact three prospects for every one proposal made. With this information, we can calculate the total effort needed to complete the four insurance sales. In this example, 36 prospects have to be developed to average 12 proposals to complete 4 sales. When this line of attack is taken with all lines of insurance, the salesperson has the ability to quantify the necessary effort for the planning process.

Incidentally, salespersons should keep track of the ratio of prospects to proposals and proposals to a sale. As they get better at their job, these ratios will improve. And, as they become more successful, the sales methodology of prospecting will blend into one based on referrals.

At the beginning of each month, the salesperson should decide how many of each activity is needed pursuant to the personal income goal. These activities would then be parceled out to each week in the planned month. At the beginning of each week, the activity list would have to be reevaluated and updated preparatory to the execution phase. The key to execution is to allot so many of each activity to each day.

155

EXECUTION

This is a rather obvious phase. Each day must be broken out by the hour or half hour, and then the activities necessary to complete the plan must be allotted time slots. All breaks or rest periods, golf, etc., should also be allotted time slots. In this case, we have taken a shortcut regarding micromeasurement. The salesperson uses his or her judgment as to length of time to allot to each task. At the end of each day, some time should be spent in evaluating the success of the plan.

If this program is followed, personal productivity will increase and so will success. It will not happen by working harder or faster, but will come about through a planned, consistent utilization of one's time—the same procedure that takes place when supervisors plan their employees' day.

Our hypothetical homemaker has not been forgotten. For this individual, the planning and execution phases are easier. A goal has to be set. For our homemaker, that goal may be to develop at least four hours of free time each day. Each day must be broken down into half- or one-hour time segments. All the work to be performed that day must be listed separately with the estimated time for completion. This list is then analyzed, and the time slots for the day are filled with the work according to the analysis. As with the salesperson, the homemaker should recap each day's plan at the end of the day as a learning technique to improve the next day's plan.

The result of this exercise is that you will be able to release that extra half person within yourself for your personal aid and benefit. And the nice part of it all is that this extra half person will not cost you anything and is not a result of working harder or faster. Productivity will improve, and it also can be fun, because now you can measure your results, which for most individuals was never possible. Since you can keep score, this whole procedure can become a game. Except, in this game you will face the toughest competition in the world—yourself.

Now a cynical comment. For every 100 people reading this chapter, I would estimate that only 1 will give it a try, and for every 10 who give it a try, only 1 will follow through. The reason for that statement is that the foundation of any work ethic (natural or planned) is personal discipline.

The Bible says that the meek shall inherit the earth. If they do, they will have to take it from the personally disciplined.

11

The Knowledge Worker and Productivity

I saved the knowledge-worker productivity issue for this position in the text because the subject becomes easier to comprehend after the reader has digested the preceding chapter on personal productivity. For the sake of emphasis, allow me to repeat some earlier comments.

"When the physicist sets out to plan these two activities, aside from preference, what is his only consideration? That there are two 30-minute time slots to fill. Nothing else matters for the simple act of measurement and planning."

"A nuclear formula can be compared to a freshly dug hole, and what we find is that, as far as elapsed time is concerned, they are the same."

The rules of productivity improvement that apply to the clerical white collar worker also hold for the knowledge worker as well as the president. The answer lies in supervision. For the president, it is personal supervision. For the knowledge worker, it is the supervisor.

Supervision and the Knowledge Worker

The basic difference between the clerical-management program outlined in this text and a knowledge-worker program is execution of the plan. In either case, the supervisor needs a complete understanding of all work in the unit. The supervisor has to plan the work against the available people. The clerical workday is usually made up of numerous work tasks, while the individual work tasks confronting the knowledge worker are not only complex and thoughtful but also time-consuming. Individual tasks can take days, weeks, and months (in the case of project work). As a result, daily work is rarely handed out to a knowledge worker. The knowledge worker receives assignments.

Let's use the assignment of project work as an example. The initial assignment process should include a joint planning session between the supervisor and knowledge worker. The result of that session should lead to a work plan/project log. The execution phase is the daily monitoring of the work plan/project log. In some cases, a weekly monitoring would be satisfactory. The monitoring session should be in-depth. The original work plan/project log should be in pencil. Invariably, a main topic of the monitoring session will be adjustments in the planned timetable. What I've just described is a rather common approach to project work.

Equally common is the lack of supervisory monitoring. The knowledge supervisor approaches supervision in the same fashion as the clerical supervisor. The knowledge supervisor prefers project work to supervision.

If you ask your knowledge supervisor for a status of project A and the answer you get is, "I'll ask Joe how he's doing," you have problems. That supervisor probably does not know the status of projects B through Z. If the supervisor doesn't, and you don't, who does?

Do you have a productivity problem?

I don't know.

The tragedy is that you don't either.

Organization, planning, execution, and control are the management answers. Macromeasurement is the control answer.

The Knowledge Worker Is Special

Three issues tend to exacerbate the white collar productivity issue as it applies to the knowledge worker.

1. The fact that a large percentage of the knowledge workers' time is think time makes it difficult to measure their workload accurately, which is necessary for planning. To plan the unit's day, you need to get control of the parts. In this case, the parts are locked in the knowledge worker's brain. They are not objective, external parts as in the clerical case. *In other words, you cannot organize or plan the knowledge workers' time without their cooperation.*

2. The average knowledge worker is better educated than clerical or blue collar workers. Quite often the knowledge worker is a college graduate; many have several degrees. The knowledge worker feels that with this formal education comes certain professional entitlements. *One major entitlement is to be able to work substantially free of supervision.*

3. The third issue that exacerbates the white collar productivity problem as it applies to knowledge workers, is that they are intelligent people. That would seem to be a strange statement. *It is the very fact that they are intelligent that allows them a more effective latitude between the poles of cooperation and noncooperation.*

These foregoing issues are further aggravated when examined in the context of the conclusion. The rules of productivity improvement that apply to a clerical white collar worker are also applicable to the knowledge worker as well as to the company president. The answer lies in a systematic approach to the

common sense basic rules of good management, i.e., organization, planning, execution, and control.

Attitude Is the Issue

I cannot overemphasize the significant part that attitude
plays in improving the knowledge worker's productivity. Increases in efficiency will come with a planned and smoothly
executed workflow. Understanding time frames is basic to
planning and execution. The key issue, therefore, is determining
time frames, i.e., 30 minutes to dig a hole, and 30 minutes to
solve a mathematical formula.

The ego of a nuclear physicist would find it difficult to let a
productivity systems installation team, which had just completed an installation with a university ground crew (occasionally ditch diggers), come to his staff and say, "You're next." The
lambs would be "baaaaing" down at Morey's till the wee hours
of the morning.

The physicist is absolutely sure his work is too technical to
be planned. Yet, the physicist at home will plan on Sunday to
dig a hole and solve a formula. Now, here's the catch—he can do
that because only he knows how long it takes to solve the
formula. Holes are sufficiently similar that their digging can be
timed. Formula-solving is all over the time spectrum.

Cooperation Is Necessary

To plan and execute the workday for knowledge workers,
you need their cooperation. Knowledge workers have a strong
feeling for the specialness and complexity of their work life. A
key point for the reader to understand is that *productivity
improvement, through planning and supervised execution, is not dependent
upon the simplicity of the activity.*

The Ultimate Example

Let's develop the ultimate example of trying to improve the productivity of a white collar individual who engages in a high technology specialty. Let's be brave. Let's take physicians and try to increase their office productivity.

I can hear it now: "Please don't interfere with my judgment about time spent per patient. I can't adhere to a schedule in the name of efficiency. After all, it took years of undergraduate and graduate work to understand the complexities of my mission. Do you think that in a couple of weeks you're going to master my profession and make me more efficient!" Physicians may regard attempts to achieve efficient output as an infringement upon their right to give each patient the time required for accurate diagnosis and care. This of course is only partially justified. It is important to use time efficiently if not for the patient's welfare, then at least for the physician's relief from a harried pace. Furthermore, an inefficient pace breeds further inefficiency, from which both patient and physician suffer. It is a relief to know that increased professional productivity has nothing to do with job complexity or working harder or faster. Increased professional productivity simply means first planning the professional's day; then, through a methodology of control, executing the plan. We can guarantee physicians the efficient use of their office day. They will be more productive.

I'll stop begging the issue. I'll take a stab at increasing the physician's office productivity. Let's say we are going to organize the physician's morning, 8 a.m. till noon. Let's say that under ideal circumstances Dr. A can handle five office visits an hour. "Oh! Putting a stopwatch to a physician?" No, physicians, like nuclear physicists, will make the time decision based on their personal knowledge. Dr. B may decide that for herself or himself four is the correct number, or six, or whatever.

We know that Dr. A can handle 5 patients an hour, or 20 patients in a morning, because the doctor tells us so. That was easy, except we qualified this plan as one that works only under ideal circumstances. Our job is to construct those ideal circumstances, just as we had to construct the work area for supervisor Mary. Then we must assign the patients out to the physician, just as Mary had to assign work. Let's make five appointments at 8 a.m., five at 9 a.m., etc. Then, let's separate the physician's office into a set of individual examining rooms. At 8 a.m. a nurse will put a patient in each room. The nurse will prepare each patient. In essence, the nurse has batched work to the doctor at one-hour intervals. The physician will proceed to each prepared patient gaining time here and losing it there, but in effect achieving the average batching with greater efficiency.

If you do not think that professionals can have their productivity optimized, notice how many people show up when you go for your next 8 a.m. appointment. And, if you think your doctor's bill is high, just think how high it would be if your physician was not organized, efficient, and productive.

I have now discussed increasing the productivity of clerical employees, knowledge workers, salespersons, homemakers, nuclear physicists, and physicians. In each case, the same basic approach applies. Why was that possible? It was possible because we are not engaged in addressing the issue of increasing their capacity to do work. The excess capacity already was there. The 4/8 Theory is a reality. We were recovering and demonstrating that capacity. We were making the intangible tangible and, therefore, manageable.

12

Should You Establish a
Productivity Department?

D oes a corporation need a productivity department? Before answering this question, let me first list what I believe are the essential productivity requisites every white collar company should be fulfilling:

1. Productivity emphasis.

2. A macroproductivity measurement system.

3. A microproductivity measurement system and the attending productivity improvement program.

4. An organized, ongoing system for maintaining, revising, and auditing productivity improvement efforts to guarantee the desired results and the durability of items two and three above. The maintenance aspect of the system ensures that the macromeasurement and micromeasurement elements are always accurate. The revision function ensures that there is a mechanism for adjusting the system to any major changes, such as the installation of data processing enhancements. The auditing feature serves as a monitoring mechanism to assure that the

productivity improvement system is being properly followed.

5. An organized unit to evaluate and install productivity improvements such as updated suggestion systems, quality circles, and other quality-of-work-life enhancements.

Professional Discipline

I can almost guarantee that any productivity improvement system you install will be quickly emasculated—unless you watch it closely and constantly. Remember my earlier descriptions of the various productivity systems as being employee-intensive or supervisory-intensive. Understand that the kind of intense, sustained attention required to ensure that such systems operate at maximum effectiveness will not be universally welcomed. A common element in the various approaches to white collar productivity improvement is the return of professional discipline to the unit, group, or individual. A common element intrinsic in companies with low productivity is the lack of professional discipline.

When I refer to discipline in this fashion, I am not referring to sanctions or punishment. I refer to personal discipline as a function of moral and professional character. If that type of discipline is in short supply, and you place within your organization a system that adjusts for this discrepancy, it follows logically that you must rather closely watch and maintain the system.

What I am saying, then, is that you do need a productivity department. I cannot say, however, whether you need such a department in addition to the organization that presently oversees corporate quality and timeliness of service. It seems to me that this is one of the reasons we are in the productivity dilemma today. For years, most companies have paid organized attention to service. Quality and timeliness are customer issues.

166

Drop the ball on either issue and you have not only your customers but also your entire sales force up in arms.

Productivity, Quality, and Service

If you drop the ball on productivity, who gets upset? No one . . . until your customers and salespersons complain about your prices and leave. No one reacts to poor productivity until your back is against the wall. In the meantime, you are concerned about quality and service on a daily basis. If your managers are harassed daily about quality and timeliness of service, what is their one out, their security blanket to keep the twin wolves of quality and timeliness away from their door?

Staffing.

Many managers solve their problems (or think they do) by throwing people at them. When was the last time you saw a budget cross your desk requesting a reduction in people count? If your managers must adapt only to the twin burdens of quality and timeliness, you can bet that the adapting will be done at least partially at the expense of productivity.

What is my point? You need a productivity department. You need a service department.

They should be one and the same: a single entity responsible for both critical functions. What you do not want is to have productivity at odds with service. If you hear this comment once, you will hear it a thousand times: "Okay, if you insist, I'll do this productivity thing, but I guarantee that our service standards will suffer. What's your phone number? I'll give it to the customers when they call."

Seasoned Talent with a Track Record

I opt for a management services department that has the responsibility for service and productivity. I recommend placing

167

an officer, or a manager of significant rank, in charge of the unit. In other words, this unit should administer its duties from a position of corporate political strength. Staff this position with seasoned talent. Don't make it a position where a manager begins a track record. Staff it initially with an individual who has corporate-wide respect.

Remember my comments regarding discipline. Usually, no one will put the welcome mat out for this unit at the operating levels of your organization, the very levels where it is needed. I know that this is illogical. No one wants to run the risk of deteriorating service or productivity. But, on a very human level, your managers may want interference even less.

Do not bury the productivity unit in your data processing organization. In a white collar atmosphere, data processing has a heavy impact on productivity. But, data processing represents an approach to the issue from an entirely different perspective. Data processing enhancements are usually welcomed.

Data processing enhancements are not grounded in people motivation and discipline. Data processing and the people productivity issues explained in this text are totally different in concept. Don't confuse them.

Presidential Backing

The productivity unit is a tough assignment that deserves top personnel with top billing. The backing of this department must originate with the president. This backing is easy to demonstrate once the macromeasurement system is installed. At that point, the president will be receiving regular reports, and he or she will know not only who is "naughty and nice" but how naughty and how nice. All the president need do is express appropriate displeasure with those units below par. The units in question will then seek out the productivity unit for help without any prompting.

I guarantee this. Why? Because the subject matter is too deep and too emotionally complicated for the offending units to extricate themselves successfully. They need the help of the productivity department. A sick doctor needs another doctor for treatment. A lawyer in legal trouble needs another lawyer. A unit in trouble cannot stand dispassionately aside and view itself. Even if it could, it could not make available the talent needed to tend itself while continuing to operate. This is why a company needs a specialized productivity department. This is also why a company needs outside help to establish the specialized department.

The Department Has To Deliver Results

One final issue: when your productivity unit is called upon to help, it had better be able and ready to help. The productivity unit should be fully trained in white collar productivity improvement systems that deliver results. If you have a unit that needs a staff of 500 employees to do a job that your competitor can handle with 300 employees, it will do no good for your productivity staff to show up at the doors of the problem unit with quality circles or a lot of theory about how Japan manages. With your competitor standing on your throat, you need immediate action. If your productivity department develops an internal reputation for delivering results, positive momentum will shift in its favor.

In summary:

1. You need an independent department responsible for productivity and service.

2. The department has to have the visible management backing that goes with internal political strength.

3. The productivity program has to have the attention of the president of your company.

4. The productivity unit must be grounded in productivity techniques that will deliver the success necessary to meet or exceed the competition. Therein lies a point that is often missed by white collar productivity theorists.

169

Quite often it seems that the basic goal of our productivity techniques is to make people happy in their jobs.

The basic goal driving productivity improvement is the need to meet and beat the competition. Granted, common sense and evidence says we are more likely to be able to do this with satisfied workers. Beyond and above that point is the moral commitment of a company to the quality-of-work-life of its employees. Yet, let's face it, what difference does it make to our workers if they have fond memories of the workplace but are standing in an unemployment line because the plant has closed for lack of orders?

13

Do You Need an
Outside Consultant?

D o you have a department that emphasizes productivity?
Do you have the internal expertise in your company to
develop a creditable productivity improvement program?

Do you have a macromeasurement system?

Do you have the expertise necessary in your company to
put into effect a creditable productivity improvement program
once you design it? In other words, can you be so dispassionate,
initially, as to answer the call, "Physician heal thyself"?

Do you understand that the availability of a creditable
productivity improvement program represents about *25 percent of
a successful battle* against low white collar productivity?

Do you understand that successfully installing a creditable
productivity improvement program in your organization, making it work with durable results, represents about *75 percent of a
successful battle* against low white collar productivity?

If you answer "No" to any of these questions, consider
outside help.

What Do You Want from a Productivity Consultant?

The services of a good white collar productivity improvement consultant are not cheap. The only expensive consultant, however, is the one who does not perform. If you decide you need outside help, then the choice of a consulting firm is obviously important. Only you can make that choice. Knowing *what* you want, however, is just as important as who. When the consultant leaves, your company should have:

1. A functioning productivity improvement organization,

2. A macromeasurement system,

3. A micromeasurement system and its supporting white collar productivity improvement program, and

4. Several installed and operating examples of item 3.

Let me elaborate on the last item. It is my opinion that the end product of a total productivity enhancement program is a stand-alone corporate productivity department. There is a great deal of advice available on the what-to-do. As the text reveals, productivity enhancement programs will not be full of mind-boggling theory. Therefore the difficult part of any program is the "how to." This is especially true with a people-oriented white collar program, even one that simply seeks to return the client units to management basics. The reason is that these programs must deal with the complexity of human emotion. As a result, every time you get involved in the "how to" of an installation, it is to some extent a new experience.

The hard part comes after your productivity organization is established and trained on a system. Now your productivity department has to produce. How to produce is the tough issue. In my opinion, the consultant's help on the "how to produce" issue is just as important as help with the "what to do" issue. And, in both cases, both issues are your ultimate responsibility. Therefore, you want it done right the first time. For that reason, keep the consultant on the job as the system is installed unit by unit until you are satisfied you can install the program successfully.

172

The Importance of Installation Training

The installation training will vary in length depending upon the productivity method you choose. It will also depend on the quality of management, supervision, and discipline in your organization. The installation training that will take the greatest length of time is the type associated with an active, supervisory-intensive program. There are two reasons for this.

1. You expect to cause results. This is always more difficult than an employee-intensive, passive program, which will probably still be awaiting results long after the consultants have left.

2. A supervisory-intensive program will not precipitate nearly as much resistance as an employee-intensive program. But, a supervisory-intensive program will generate a high level of quality interest. Therefore, the program is constantly reacting and adapting to the legitimate concerns of management.

Management Commitment

Let me close this section with an elaboration on the subject of quality of management, supervision, and general discipline. *It is highly unlikely that any consultant, or your own productivity department using whatever program, can install a productivity improvement system and have it rise above the managerial competence and/or commitment of the client or unit in question.* This is particularly true of knowledge-worker units. American management abdicated supervisory control of these units long ago. The fundamentals of management, organization, planning, execution, and control must return to the knowledge-worker units. A consultant can tell you what to do and how to do it. But this advice will be wasted on any management group that is not willing to assert itself.

If you are considering hiring a consulting firm, know what you want.

173

14

Management:
The Productivity Solution

L et's discuss why management represents the key to the productivity problem. This discussion is in addition to the much discussed management problems of research and development funding, shortsighted profit planning versus long-range (strategic) planning, and so on. I am going to discuss management's failure to manage its people. This is an important issue to identify so that we can avoid repetition of the problem. The answer to it falls into these categories:

1. Productivity Awareness

This issue is being amply addressed today through the national attention productivity is receiving. I wrote this book to drive home the point that no company, no success-oriented individual can stand aloof from the issue of productivity. As I have said repeatedly, if you ignore the problem and your competition doesn't, you might as well close your doors, because eventually they will be closed for you.

2. Delegation of Authority and Responsibility

Obviously, the delegation of authority and responsibility pertains to a broad spectrum of issues, not just productivity. We are not going to solve our productivity dilemma, however, until we realize that responsibility for its solution lies at every level of the organization.

Simply stated, the act of management should be exercised through a chain of delegated authority and responsibility. I am not going to discuss overlapping chains of delegation, i.e., solid and dotted lines. I am not going to try to legitimize the current state of managerial art with the term "matrix." I am simply going straight for the managerial jugular. One of our national management problems is that we delegate authority and abdicate responsibility.

As managers, we tend to confuse giving direction with delegation. Our problem is not that we fail to give direction but that we fail to exercise control over the direction given. Telling someone to do something is not necessarily managing the doing. I have always been amazed that managers could give direction and then not be interested enough in the issue in question to stay on top of it.

In other words, we all recognize that our corporate lives are too complex to personally manage all the issues we delegate, but we do have the obligation to exercise control over all those issues we delegated. We are not now doing so. Managers are giving directions and then they are walking away from the responsibility of the directive. Walking away from a directive is difficult when you are the next level above the directive's execution phase, but even then it occurs all too often. The walking away becomes more complete as intervening layers of management isolate the particular manager.

This has gone on so long that cause and effect are now lost. Needless to say, the condition of white collar productivity in the United States today is embarrassing. We glibly impute the problem to our frontline employees. Conveniently, the problem leaves no traceable tracks through our management ranks, and therefore no identifiable responsibility.

My point is that all the king's productivity departments and all the king's productivity improvement systems will not put our productivity Humpty Dumpty back together again without meaningful responsibility and commitment at every level of the organization.

3. The Productivity Department

Productivity enhancements are currently being incorrectly incorporated structurally into the average American company. When you bring a productivity inprovement program to a company, you get immediate attention at each end of the company hierarchy. The president is interested because he or she probably spotlighted productivity improvement as a company issue. At the opposite pole are the individuals who know that they will get stuck implementing the program; needless to say, you have their attention.

In between, you have a spectrum of casual interest. Many of the intermediate layers of management would prefer that the whole matter of productivity improvement just go away. Unless you watch it carefully, it eventually will. Many of these managers view a productivity improvement system as an undoing of their years of labor or, worse yet, a possible indictment of their adminstration. Strange as it may seem, few managers see it as an opportunity to improve their operations. Too often, productivity management is viewed, to use a current buzzword, as voodoo management. That is one reason I wrote this book. If you do not understand the theory and logic of a concept, why would you rush to embrace it?

Typically, a company embraces productivity improvement as a crusade. An individual is selected to head up this crusade. The president delegates to this individual the responsibility to increase company productivity; authority can't be delegated, because this individual fills a staff role. What happens now is that, instead of incorporating productivity responsibility into the structure of the organization, the company tacks it on like a malignant appendage. The chosen individual then surveys a number of outside consulting firms to determine the proper approach to the company's productivity problem. He or she chooses an appropriate system and, with the consulting firm, sets up a productivity department.

Now it's time to execute. The productivity manager goes to Division A and finds that, for that division, the timing is wrong. Division B is unique; it won't work there. Division C has already tried something similar, and it didn't work. Division D is under the cloud of a union threat. Division E never liked the productivity manager in the first place and will not give him or her the time of day. Division F has all new employees; come back later.

Guess where the productivity manager goes next? To the marketing department so that she or he can develop a marketing package to sell productivity to the divisions. Now comes the awareness campaign. Unfortunately, Divisions A through F see through this fast footwork. They counter with the rumor that the productivity department ordered a gross of red armbands with black swastikas. The president throws up his or her hands and fixes on a new crusade.

What was the problem?

The president should have delegated the responsibility and the authority for companywide improved productivity to the executive vice president . . . with collateral goals and controls (to ensure responsibility). The executive vice president should have delegated the same authority and responsibility, with the same intensity of control, to the divisional vice presidents. This delegation should have proceeded in the same frank, intense, and controlled fashion right down to the unit supervisor.

At the same time, the president should have announced that, because the issue of productivity is as complex as it is, the president was establishing a department as a resource, to which the divisions and units could turn for help. As a staff department, its primary function would be to give systems and installation help. Responsibility for productivity achievement lies with the executive vice president, vice presidents, and so on, through the divisions and units in question. The macromeasurement system would keep the president's hand firmly on the control and responsibility issue. She or he can be certain of a "responsible" delegation of authority.

The productivity department manager's head would be on the line to deliver real and substantive help. One division receiving substantive help is worth 10 awareness campaigns.

The key to productivity success, once you have the correct tools, is keeping the collective corporate feet to the fire for results, and the way to do this is through good management.

APPENDIX ONE

Strategic Planning Application Of Productivity Measurement

INTRODUCTION

Firms employ strategic planning to evaluate their future competitive position and formulate goals as they relate to that position. Even more than that, they use it to ensure their long-term market survival. Strategic planning implies longrun decisions—decisions that are more enduring and consequently more difficult to correct once a misjudgment is made. Because of its scope, strategic planning has become one of the most vital exercises of decision-making that top executives participate in. Through these exercises, they find answers to the basic questions "What are we currently doing?" and "What should we be doing?" It is through this analysis that a company defines its mission, its *raison d'être*.

It is also during this strategic planning session that top management identifies the navigational route for tactical decisions by setting general objectives for the operational issues. They address such objectives as:

- Profits
- Sales
- Cash Flow
- Marketing
- Capital Acquisition
- Resource Utilization
- Production

They mesh these objectives to enable the firm to fulfill its defined mission; and to a private enterprise, this is essentially tied to maintaining or attaining a desired level of profitability. When these objectives are set, performance is thereafter monitored to ensure conformity with the broad corporate plan.

This appendix addresses a different facet of strategic planning by revealing a hidden issue seldom considered in the formulation of corporate plans. A gap exists in current planning methodologies—a gap that may affect a company's long-term profitability and ultimately its long-term survival.

182

In order to understand this issue, consider the following example of a strategic plan. Given a mission to retain market leadership, a company's management may establish a strategic plan to increase its sales revenue by 20 percent over a period of 5 years. With this objective, the firm is expected to retain market leadership measured in total dollar sales. A related objective is to set a 20-percent expense-growth limit for capital acquisition and resource utilization. Since both revenue and expenses are to grow at the same rate, such a plan (if realistic) should enable the firm to retain its current level of profitability. This may be true only in the shortrun, however.

In the example given, the company monitors progress in terms of revenue over expenses. This gives a profitability measure. But understand that revenue comprises units sold and unit prices. How is revenue expected to grow? Is the company to achieve this by increasing price or by increasing the company's market share (the true share expressed in units sold)? On the expense side, how do you plan to manage expenses to the 20-percent level? Do you maintain the proportion of resources to units sold or do you expect the price of resources to go down? Since profitability will seemingly gain either way, does it matter how you derive your gains?

It does matter. Unless you do further analysis, you may be misled to assume that increased profits in the shortrun equate to a properly executed plan.

We live in an environment in which one firm attempts to outsell its competitor in the hope of garnering a larger share of a product's market. This ability to compete is a company's assurance of survival. But a company can sell more only if its product can be consistently priced lower than its competitor's product of equivalent quality. It seems apparent, then, that you must attempt to sell a product at the lowest price affordable. This applies even in markets with few competitors or monopolies, because at some point overpriced products that produce high profits are bound to attract new, aggressive competition. Since companies producing the same products more than likely consume the same kinds of resources, one can assume the trend in unit costs (inflation rate) for the resources is consistent in the industry. If this is true, where is the competitive edge? How can one company gain over another? How can a company consistently have lower priced products without perpetually losing money?

Consider this premise:

In the long term, safe profitability gains can only come from increases in productivity.

The only answer is productivity: using proportionally fewer resources to make the product. Does this premise appear to be simplistic? It isn't. Management has only recently learned how to define and measure productivity. Therefore, the premise is difficult to apply.

Even today, in spite of the increased popularity of the productivity issue, measurement is still in its infancy. Because of the large investment required, very few firms have established total-factor productivity measurement systems for their whole operations. As a result, productivity measurement has not had the opportunity to evolve into more advanced applications.

Coming back to the original premise, if we can achieve long-term gains only through productivity increases, then to plan and set long-term goals, a profit-oriented company must consider its future productivity position. Take this one step further and you have moved from the realm of productivity diagnostics into the arena of productivity goal-setting, or *planning*.

Productivity goal-setting establishes the link between strategic planning and productivity. Using the technique of total-factor productivity measurement, a new kind of planning model was developed and validated. In contrast to building a productivity measurement system, developing this strategic planning model does not require a large investment and is a practical tool for upper management. I explain the theory behind the model below. There then follows a case study to show how an actual working model was built for an insurance company.

THE FRAMEWORK

In order for a strategic plan to reflect a true evaluation of a company's condition, it must involve productivity measurement; measurement becomes the framework.

First, let's briefly review some basic productivity measurement principles as described in chapter four. To build a total-factor productivity measurement system (one that considers labor, materials, energy, and capital), we must begin by reviewing the company's standard income statement. We extrapolate measures from this financial report to reveal a unique approach to performance analysis. An example of such a performance measure is shown in figure A-1.

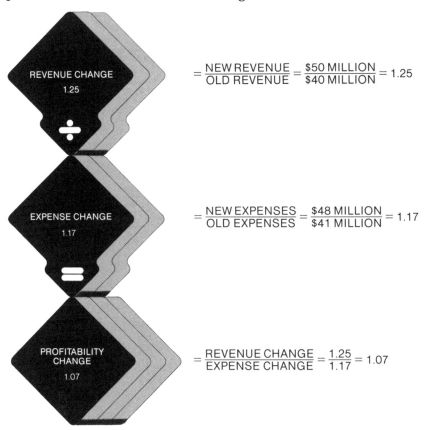

$$= \frac{\text{NEW REVENUE}}{\text{OLD REVENUE}} = \frac{\$50\,\text{MILLION}}{\$40\,\text{MILLION}} = 1.25$$

$$= \frac{\text{NEW EXPENSES}}{\text{OLD EXPENSES}} = \frac{\$48\,\text{MILLION}}{\$41\,\text{MILLION}} = 1.17$$

$$= \frac{\text{REVENUE CHANGE}}{\text{EXPENSE CHANGE}} = \frac{1.25}{1.17} = 1.07$$

Figure A-1

185

The income statement displays the traditional *financial value* relationship of outputs to inputs. One can use this report to analyze

Revenue Change = the change in financial value of the output

Expense Change = the change in financial value of the input.

By comparing the trends of these two elements, we can identify a financial performance measure: *profitability change.* In the figure A-1 example, profitability increased 7 percent.

We can take the analysis a step further. Using the basic accounting information needed to compute revenues and expenses, we can subdivide each value change into its driving components, a price change and a quantity change. (See figure A-2.)

We compute the change-ratios for physical quantities and unit prices in the same way as we do the financial values. For example, change in product quantity sold is the ratio of the new quantity sold to the old quantity sold.

$$\text{Product Quantity Change} = \frac{\text{New Quantity}}{\text{Old Quantity}} = \frac{1{,}100 \text{ Units}}{1{,}000 \text{ Units}} = 1.1$$

The combination of the product quantity change of 10 percent and the unit price change of 14 percent results in a 25-percent change in revenue. The 17-percent change in expenses was due to a 2-percent increase in resources used and a 15-percent increase in the unit cost of those resources.

We can then extrapolate two new performance ratios that are basic to the strategic planning model: *productivity change* and *price recovery change.* The chart in figure A-3 on page 188 displays how each is developed.

This familiar representation of productivity measurement is the basis of a strategic planning model.

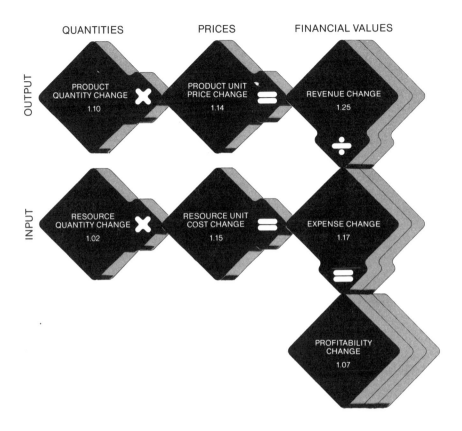

Figure A-2

Each box in the chart in figure A-3 relates mathematically to several other variables. With the knowledge of some of the change-ratios (established as goals, trends, or forecasts), we can compute the missing factors. This is the point of departure from productivity monitoring to planning. Through trial and error, a manager can very easily test the impact of changes in prices, quantities, and profit objectives. Each computation yields a planned productivity and price recovery change, which we can separately analyze and relate to long-term strategic plans. This makes the model an excellent arena for resolving "what if . . ." questions.

187

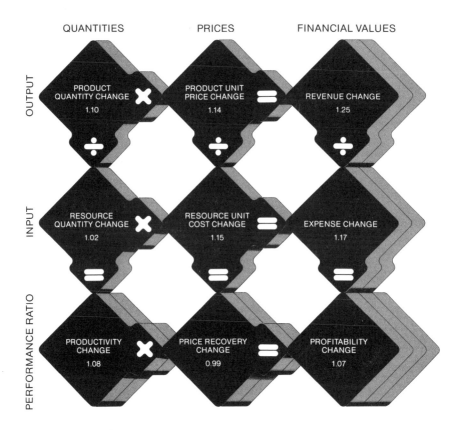

Figure A-3

The performance ratios of profitability, productivity, and price recovery become key indices in the development of the model. Here is a brief explanation of each one:

• **Profitability change**—Addresses the change in the relationship of revenue to expenses. The ratio is familiar to those who frequently analyze financial statements as a reflection of a change in ROI (Return on Investment). A ratio of 1.0 reflects a status quo. When the ratio exceeds unity, there is a gain in the ROI. A ratio of less than 1.0 warns that expenses are growing at a faster rate than revenue. Profitability reflects the *combined* impact of changes in productivity and price recovery. It is a financial performance measure.

● **Productivity change**—Tracks the change in the relationship of the quantity sold of the product to the quantity of resources consumed. Productivity is the trump card in the game of market competition, because it is the only safe source of long-term profits.

Productivity can increase through improvement in either of two components, *efficiency* and *capacity utilization.* Efficiency increases when the proportional amount of resources consumed to make the product is reduced. This results from better management of resources and technological innovations affecting the utilization of resources. If resources are fixed such that its quantity cannot be manipulated, gains in productivity can still be achieved by addressing the output side of the formula, i.e., increasing production. This component of productivity is capacity utilization. Since a company would normally have its resources divided into those that are variable and those that are fixed, the combination of efficiency and capacity utilization determines total productivity. Deciding where to focus one's attention in the productivity index (production vs. resource utilization) should be based on the proportion of fixed resources to variable resources; i.e., if the fixed assets are dominant, set increasing output as the overriding priority over decreasing inputs.

● **Price Recovery Change**—Focuses on the change in the relationship of product unit prices to resource unit costs. This ratio reveals the impact of market forces and inflation. Since the prices of resources consumed are normally (in a competitive industry) beyond a company's control, price recovery shows if product prices are moving faster or slower than the inflation rate of resources consumed. All other things held constant, if a firm wishes to retain its market, it will price at the lowest possible rate it can afford. For the industry, this is a price recovery ratio of 1.0, which means prices are increased in direct proportion to the inflation rate of the cost of the resources used. A ratio greater than 1.0 implies greater profits in the shortrun with a potential loss in market share over the longrun. A ratio less than 1.0 means initially reduced profits but possibly more market penetration. A company can even finance a price recovery ratio of less than 1.0 (in the interest of more aggressive competition) by increased productivity.

The model shown is oversimplified to make the point. In an actual situation, you cannot relate revenue and expense to profitability unless you consider all product lines and all expenses. In the case-study section, there is a more realistic example of a total-factor productivity measurement system in use for planning. Total-factor measurement has normally been a complex process, primarily because it requires a variety of data. For use as a planning tool, however, change-ratios effectively reduce the need for a large volume of data.

As you will see later, this model is *not* a substitute for your current planning methodology; it simply expands it. Managers still have to analyze the interrelationships of many variables just as they've always done. For example, its methodology does not address the dependency of units sold to unit price; you must understand not only that price increases above the inflation rate can have a negative impact on sales growth, but also that additional concepts such as elasticity of demand exist. The point is, if you link this model to your current planning techniques, you will get fresh insight into your analysis by answering the question "Where do my profits really come from?"

LONG-TERM SECTOR ANALYSIS

Profitability, productivity, and price recovery as defined here are new terms to most. By analyzing the combination of trends in these measures, you can evaluate your company's long-term prospects. Some of these combinations of performance ratios may reveal unexpected results. It is easy to understand why increasing productivity improves a company's position.

It is not as obvious, however, why decreasing profitability may not necessarily imply trouble.

The Long-Term Sector Analysis chart (see figure A-4) provides a quick summary of the effects of various performance ratio trend combinations.

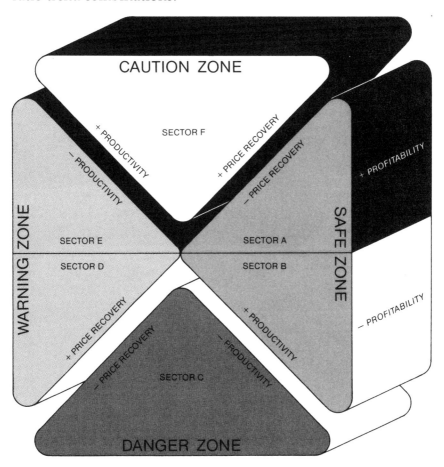

Figure A-4

Each triangular area in figure A-4 is marked as a sector. A sector falls into one of four zones, which serves to underscore the seriousness of the long-term implications. Notice from the chart in figure A-4 that a company experiencing profitability gains (upper half of chart) may still be in the caution or warning zones. On the other hand, a company may have decreasing profitability (lower half of chart) and yet be secure in the long term.

In order to point out the implications of each long-term sector, there follows a brief description of each one.

Sector A

- Increasing Productivity
- Decreasing Price Recovery
- Increasing Profitability

This is the preferred strategic sector, because productivity gains are planned to finance a level of product prices that will be lower than the industry's prices. Typically, productivity increases are expected to be substantial, since profitability will also improve. If other companies cannot manage to increase productivity at a significant rate, the sector A company will be impossible to catch. This strategy provides an extra windfall in that lower prices encourage market-share gain. Matched by an increase in production, this would improve capacity utilization of fixed resources, thus assuring continued productivity improvement.

Sector B

- Increasing Productivity
- Decreasing Price Recovery
- Decreasing Profitability

Sector B placement implies two possibilities. It can show pricing aggressiveness to the extent of using cutthroat tactics. If a company has a big pool of profits to take from and productivity increases are substantial, then this strategy can drive the competition out of the market. Should this aggressive gamble pan out, the eventual gain in market share will result in substantial gains in capacity utilization, which should subsequently redirect the profitability trend upward.

If a less aggressive company plans to be in this sector, it should consider adjusting its pricing as it is not gaining enough in productivity to finance the strategy. Overall it is easy to change direction from this sector back to sector A.

Sector C

- Decreasing Productivity
- Decreasing Price Recovery
- Decreasing Profitability

All the performance ratios are trending downward. This is not a healthy direction for a strategic plan. A company following this path is unlikely to survive. The primary reason why a firm is headed in this direction could be that it has established the product price level much too high, so it is attempting to reduce its price significantly. But this strategy reveals that the company can no longer attract enough customers; at least not enough customers to increase capacity utilization and thus maintain productivity. Possibly, this company has such substantial fixed costs that it has become inflexible. Perhaps a competitor attracted by the past high profits and high prices has finally taken control of the market. If a company ends up with these trends in performance ratios, it will be too late to react.

Sector D

- Decreasing Productivity
- Increasing Price Recovery
- Decreasing Profitability

This sector falls into the warning zone. Costly reductions in productivity are being covered up by price increases. Be wary of employing this strategy. The increasing price recovery will leave its tracks in the longrun when the demand for the product goes down and capacity utilization becomes a serious concern. If productivity has not been substantially reduced, this sector implies a moderate price recovery increase. This company will need to address productivity to get back on the right track and prevent further erosion of its long-term profitability. It should carefully evaluate its pricing approach.

Sector E

- Decreasing Productivity
- Increasing Price Recovery
- Increasing Profitability

This is the final stage before reaching the hopeless state of sector C, a very dangerous position. It represents the last warning. Placement in this sector suggests that the company is planning to make short-term gains solely through price increases. Even then, part of the short-term profits are expected to be eroded by productivity problems. Situations such as these will attract new competitors. Slowly, market share will be reduced and productivity will become an even more serious concern because of underutilized capacity. The company must address productivity *now* to prevent this situation from deteriorating further. This sector implies rapid increases in pricing recovery, much more so than sector D, since profitability is increasing. This is the worst source of profitability gains.

Sector F

- Increasing Productivity
- Increasing Price Recovery
- Increasing Profitability

This sector is the biggest source of short-term profits. And, as with any strategy that uses the pricing umbrella, it will attract new competition. If this approach is followed in the long term, a capacity utilization problem may result from a loss in market share. It is encouraging, though, that a course such as this can be corrected quickly if competitors begin to penetrate the market; the company can fall back on its productivity increase. But the guiding word here is *caution.*

An important thing to remember is that the analysis shown deals only with the long term. It is quite possible for a company to use a sector D strategy in the short term with a plan to offset its impact with a sector B strategy at some later point.

Also, Long-Term Sector Analysis addresses change over time, rather than a level of performance. This means a company as opportunistic in the short term and historically has proved to be profitable. Its automobile insurance operation is divided into four divisions, each of which is responsible for a particular territory. These are:

- Northern Region
- Southern Region
- Eastern Region
- Western Region

Each division has several branch offices. A separate management group is responsible for the total operation in each divisional territory. These management teams report directly to the chief operating officer at the home office.

Several functional staff members also report to the chief operating officer. These are the planning, actuarial, administrative services, and insurance administration officers, all of whom serve in an advisory capacity to the field as well as manage home office operations.

The company has always emphasized increasing productivity and, for this reason, it has achieved remarkable growth.

After we established a productivity measurement system, we saw that ABC was the ideal setting for developing a strategic planning model.

3. Definition of Variables

The variables described in the productivity measurement model are generic. In order to illustrate its application in insurance, we evaluated the variables and replaced them with equivalent insurance-industry terms. Where applicable, we also developed weighting procedures. You will find a definition of each of these insurance variables below:

Revenue, Expense, and Profitability

Certain industries have easily defined profitability measures. Manufacturing companies are a good example. Their revenue is the gross income they derive from the sales of tangible products, and their expenses represent the financing of the resources used. These revenue and expense figures, which are directly identified in the financial

197

statements, provide an ROI measure. You can pit the trend of this measure against competitors to determine your comparative financial performance.

In the financial services sector, however, businesses cannot directly derive such ROI measures from their income statements; it is a much more complex matter. This probably explains why financial institutions lag behind other industries in developing productivity measures. One reason for the complexity is the inherent difficulty of defining a financial institution's products and resources. The financial statements themselves do not clearly display the inputs and outputs. A commercial bank, for example, derives income from interest on loans; clearly a revenue item. On the other hand, the bank also pays interest on savings and time deposits. Is this an expense item? Not necessarily. In one approach, planners use the margin between interest income and interest expense as a revenue item and make a ratio of this figure against all other standard resources (labor, overhead, etc.) to determine ROI. This way, the current level of interest rates does not distort the ROI figure.

We can identify a similar situation in our insurance company case. We can say that an insurance company's purpose is to maintain a fund out of which those who suffer losses may be reimbursed. The fund belongs to those individuals who share the risk and pay premiums. The company derives income from that portion of premium not allocated to the benefits fund, and this serves as a reimbursement for the cost of maintenance services and a return for putting its capital at risk.

Revenue and expenses for an insurance company are normally represented in this manner:

i)   Revenue = Premium

        = Pure Premium* + Income from Processing Services

ii) Expense = Losses Incurred + Processing Expenses.

---

* Pure Premium in this case is the amount provided for expected claims losses.

The inverse ratio of revenue and expense as defined here relates to a commonly used profitability measure in insurance, better known as the composite ratio. For purposes of a strategic planning model, the composite ratio does not provide enough information for monitoring financial performance, so a new measure was developed.

Since an insurance company's goal is to maintain enough premium in the fund to cover all the losses, we can assume that over time, the ratio of pure premium to losses incurred should equal one, i.e., the amount provided for projected losses will equal actual losses. Of course, this is not always true in the shortrun since projections reflect an expected average. This would also be affected by midterm changes in underwriting programs. In the longrun, however, insurance companies will project the *same* pure premium for the *same* market. Since a company, on the average, performs at the same level with respect to losses when compared with other similar companies, the ratio of pure premium to losses incurred is not a measure that reveals its performance within a market peer group. It is not an area where one company gains over its competitors. To identify the values subject to market competition, one must identify the factors that make one company differ from another. This was accomplished by removing the impact of losses and representing revenue, expense, and profitability in this manner:

i)   Revenue*   = Premium − Pure Premium
                    = Income from Processing Services

ii) Expenses   = Processing Expenses

---

* Note that I did not explain investment income, dividends, and other statutory adjustments, in the interests of simplicity; I incorporated these as an adjustment to the pure premium figure.

Profitability, or ROI, will therefore be defined as follows:

$$\text{Profitability} = \frac{\text{Revenue}}{\text{Expense}} = \frac{\text{Income from Processing Services}}{\text{Processing Expenses}}$$

Those familiar with other measurement techniques will notice a similarity of income for processing services with the value-added method.

199

Product Quantity

A good measure of the product of an insurance company is the insurance policy. It is the service contract of the company with the insured, assuring the individual that the proper share of benefits will be provided when required and that accurate records are maintained. We can define the volume of the product as the number of insurance policies in force, since this quantity approximates the volume of services to be provided.

A multiple product/market company needs to apply a weighting system that reflects the varying degrees of effort required to process or support different products, such as different kinds of insurance policies. Productivity measurement experts generally agree that in change analysis, price weighting is a sound method of accounting for product differences. Price weighting assumes that product prices reflect to a large degree the relative differences in production effort. In our more complicated insurance example, however, this is not necessarily the case. Product price (premium per policy) reflects factors other than those related to processing effort. In fact, a big portion of the price reflects the provision for expected benefit payments. By eliminating this from the price, we can determine the processing expense per policy. This more accurately represents the relative differences in effort required by different products and is used as the weights.

We devised the chart in table A-1 to compute weights. In this particular company, products differ from one territory to another in response to varying state insurance laws. Therefore, we weighted by territory. The final weights are each territory's percentage share of total processing expenses.

In table A-2, you see how to apply computed weights to policy count change-ratios to determine the final weighted change.

Table A-1
COMPUTING POLICY COUNT WEIGHTS

TERRITORY	CURRENT $ PREMIUM*		EXPENSE RATIO		PROCESSING EXPENSE $*	WEIGHTS % TO TOTAL PROC. EXPENSE		
1. *Northern Region*	44.2	X	.302	=	13.35	28.5 %		
2. *Southern Region*	21.2	X	.297	=	8.08	17.2 %		
3. *Eastern Region*	24.6	X	.257	=	6.33	13.5 %		
4. *Western Region*	70.2	X	.272	=	19.10	40.8 %		
				TOTAL	46.86	100.0 %		

*In millions

Table A-2
WEIGHTING POLICY COUNT CHANGE

TERRITORY		WEIGHTS % TO TOTAL PROC. EXPENSE		CHANGE IN POLICY COUNT	
1. *Northern Region*		28.5 % X		0.90 =	.257
2. *Southern Region*		17.2 % X		1.07 =	.184
3. *Eastern Region*		13.5 % X		1.04 =	.140
4. *Western Region*		40.8 % X		1.02 =	.416
	TOTAL	100.0 %		WEIGHTED CHANGE	.997

roduct Price

Normally one thinks of a product's price as the final selling price; for an insurance policy, it is the average premium per policy. In this particular application we are concerned only with the processing portion of the price. Therefore, we excluded the portion of the price provisioned as pure premium or expected losses. Thus:

Processing Price = Average Premium per Policy – Average Pure Premium per Policy

Rather than deal specifically with the processing price, for purposes of familiarity and ease of computation, we weighted the average premium and average pure premium figures separately.

For weighting prices (either the total price or the pure premium portion), we used a technique called quantity weighting. This technique reflects the future mix of business.

The weighting example shown in table A-3 illustrates the computations we used in weighting average premium. We converted the current premiums by product territory to their expected future value, assuming no price change. We did this by multiplying each premium figure by the corresponding policy count change-ratios that had been projected. The resulting value is called future premium. Each territory's percentage share of the future premium serves as the weight.

Table A-4 is an example of weighting with change-ratios for prices applied.

We use a similar procedure to compute a weighted pure premium per policy change. The only difference is that we replace the future premium figures with pure premium.

Resource Quantities and Resource Prices

In order to identify the different resources used by an insurance company to provide customer services, we reviewed the company's operating statement. We defined 15

Table A-3
COMPUTING PRODUCT PRICE WEIGHTS

TERRITORY	CURRENT $ PREMIUM*		CHANGE IN POLICY COUNT		FUTURE $ PREMIUM*	WEIGHTS % TO TOTAL FUTURE PREMIUM		
1. Northern Region	44.2	X	0.90	=	39.8	24.0 %		
2. Southern Region	27.2	X	1.07	=	29.1	17.5 %		
3. Eastern Region	24.6	X	1.04	=	25.6	15.4 %		
4. Western Region	70.2	X	1.02	=	71.6	43.1 %		
				TOTAL	166.1	100.0 %		

*In millions

Table A-4
WEIGHTING PRODUCT PRICE CHANGE

TERRITORY		WEIGHTS % TO TOTAL FUTURE PREMIUM		CHANGE IN PRICE		
1. Northern Region		24.0	% X	1.05	=	.252
2. Southern Region		17.5	% X	1.01	=	.177
3. Eastern Region		15.4	% X	1.09	=	.168
4. Western Region		43.1	% X	1.14	=	.491
	TOTAL	100.0	%	WEIGHTED CHANGE		1.088

203

general categories of expenses. Then, we separated each category into a unit cost and quantity component. For example, we broke down salaries into employee full-time equivalents (quantity) and wage per employee (unit cost).

In the insurance industry, or in the financial services sector in general, such an analysis is not always so straightforward. This becomes evident when dealing with expense items that do not relate to physical resources—for example, premium taxes. We broke premium taxes into policies in force (quantity) and tax per policy (unit cost). Policies in force are not normally thought of as a resource. For monetary resources, however, we wanted simply to separate the inflationary element from the expense item. The complete analysis of the expense categories is shown in table A-5.

For purposes of the planning model, our task was to track the unit cost and quantity change of each of these items. Realistically, the amount of data required makes that a difficult task. In fact, closer review of the data showed that in order to do this, we needed an even more detailed breakdown. For planning purposes, the gain of mathematical exactness did not offset the effort required, so we devised a shortcut.

We segmented the expense items into groups where one can logically see items change at the same rate. Within each group we identified a general indicator. An example of such a grouping is the change in building space and desk equipment. We assumed that if the company were to expand its building space by 5 percent, other things being equal, it would also increase its desk equipment by 5 percent.

For resource quantity change, we computed four basic indicators and their impact on the total expense. These are:

i) Policies in force

ii) Branch employee count

Table A-5
BREAKDOWN OF EXPENSES INTO PRICE AND QUANTITY

EXPENSE ITEM	=	RESOURCE QUANTITY	X	RESOURCE UNIT COST
1. Commissions		1. Active agents		1. Commission per agent
2. Advertising		2. Advertisements		2. Cost per ad
3. Agency expense		3. Agency FTE's		3. Wage per FTE
4. Salaries (Branch)		4. Branch FTE's		4. Wage per FTE
5. Payroll taxes/ Benefits (Branch)		5. Branch FTE's		5. Benefits per FTE
6. Building		6. Square feet of building space		6. Rent per square foot
7. Printing & Stationery		7. Documents		7. Cost per document
8. Postage		8. Postal items		8. Postage rate
9. Motor vehicle reports		9. Reports ordered		9. Cost per report
10. Telephone		10. Calls		10. Charge per call
11. Salaries/Benefits (H.O.)		11. H.O. FTE's		11. Wages & Benefits per FTE
12. Equipment (HQ)		12. Equipment		12. Average cost of equipment
13. Data processing		13. Computer capacity		13. Cost per unit capacity
14. Travel		14. Trips		14. Cost per trip
15. Premium taxes		15. Policies in force		15. Tax per policy

FTE EQUATES TO FULL-TIME EQUIVALENT EMPLOYEES.

iii) Home office employee count

iv) Square feet of building space.

The grouping used for each quantity indicator is shown in table A-6 on the following page.

Table A-6

RESOURCE QUANTITY INDICATORS

Indicator	Expense Category	Quantity Measure	% To Total Expense
1. Policies in force	(a) Commission	(a) Active agents	55.0%
	(b) Agency expense	(b) Agency FTE's	1.9
	(c) Telephone	(c) Calls	1.6
	(d) Printing & stationery	(d) Documents printed	1.4
	(e) Postage	(e) Postal items	3.6
	(f) Motor vehicle reports	(f) Reports ordered	3.1
	(g) Premium taxes	(g) Policies in force	8.0
			74.6%
2. Branch employees	(a) Salaries	(a) FTE's—Branch	6.6%
	(b) Payroll taxes & benefits	(b) FTE's—Branch	2.0
	(c) Travel	(c) Trips—Branch	0.4
			9.0%
3. Home office employees	(a) Salaries, benefits, travel, payroll taxes (allocations)	(a) FTE's—Home office	7.9%
			7.9%
4. Square feet of building space	(a) Building	(a) Square feet of building space	3.1%
	(b) Advertising	(b) Ads.	1.8
	(c) Data processing equipment	(c) Computer capacity	2.6
	(d) Equipment (Home office allocation)	(d) Equipment	1.0
			8.5%

We used the percentage share of total expenses affected by each indicator as the weight applied to the indicator. Note that some of the expense categories may have no relationship at all to the group indicator. If the item's share of total expenses was small, we placed it in the group that would change within the same general range.

We chose the indicators according to the varying degrees of change that could occur among various resource quantities. For example "policies in force" aptly describes the trend in resources that move proportionally with output. Postal items, for instance, normally increase in direct proportion to the increase in insurance policies. This does

206

not mean, however, that resource quantities always move with the indicator. If the planner believes that during the planning period a technological innovation is going to allow the company to combine several mailings into one (which would result in postage savings), then the planner may decide to alter the change-ratio associated with policies in force.

"Square feet of building space" describes fixed resources or items that seldom change. Employee counts, however, relate to more controllable resources. We divided these into home office and branch to relate the expenses to the responsible management groups.

We made a similar attempt at grouping to track the change in unit cost of each resource. Again we identified four basic inflation indicators:

  i)   Wages per employee FTE,

  ii) Average premium per policy,

  iii) Wholesale price index, and

  iv) Rent per square foot of building space.

The detail grouping and the corresponding share of total expenses are shown in table A-7 on the following page.

Note that these variables are only indicators. On occasion they may no longer reflect an actual change in the expense items. If this occurs, a reevaluation of the indicators is necessary.

Using resource quantity and price indicators that have just been developed, one can now compute weighted change. See tables A-8 and A-9 on page 209.

The Complete Insurance Model

We had finally defined all the variables for the insurance model. The productivity measurement model of ABC Insurance, with applicable variables, is shown in figure A-5 on page 210.

207

Table A-7

RESOURCE PRICE INDICATORS

Indicator	Expense Category	Price Measure	% To Total Expense
1. Wages per FTE	(a) Branch salaries	(a) Wages per FTE	6.6%
	(b) Branch payroll taxes & benefits	(b) Benefits per FTE	2.0
	(c) Agency expense	(c) Wages per FTE	1.9
	(d) Travel	(d) Trips	0.4
	(e) Home office salaries, benefits, travel	(e) Cost per FTE	7.9
			18.8%
2. Average premium per policy	(a) Commissions	(a) Commission per active agent	55.0%
	(b) Premium taxes	(b) Tax per policy	8.0
			63.0%
3. Wholesale price index	(a) Postage	(a) Postage rate	3.6%
	(b) Motor vehicle reports	(b) Cost per report	3.1
	(c) Telephone	(c) Charge per call	1.6
	(d) Advertising	(d) Cost per ad.	1.8
	(e) Printing & stationery	(e) Cost per document	1.4
			11.5%
4. Rent per square foot	(a) Building	(a) Rent per square foot	3.1%
	(b) Equipment (allocations)	(b) Average cost of equipment	1.0
	(c) Data processing equipment	(c) Cost per unit capacity	2.6
			6.7%

To facilitate the planning process, we translated the chart identifying the variables (figure A-5) into a worksheet. This is shown in figure A-6 on page 211. The worksheet starts with variables already familiar to insurance management. We inserted formulas under each variable to display the various ways to compute a value, assuming this is not given. By identifying as few as four given values, you can simulate the effect on profitability, productivity, and price recovery.

Table A-8
WEIGHTING RESOURCE QUANTITY CHANGE

RESOURCE QUANTITY INDICATORS		WEIGHTS % TO TOTAL EXPENSES		RESOURCE QUANTITY CHANGE	
1. Policies in force		74.6	% X	1.10 =	.821
2. Branch employees		9.0	% X	0.95 =	.086
3. Home office employees		7.9	% X	0.95 =	.075
4. Square feet of building space		8.5	% X	1.00 =	.085
	TOTAL	100.0	%	WEIGHTED CHANGE	1.067

Table A-9
WEIGHTING RESOURCE UNIT COST CHANGE

RESOURCE UNIT COST INDICATORS		WEIGHTS % TO TOTAL* EXPENSES		RESOURCE UNIT COST CHANGE	
1. Wage per hour		18.8	% X	1.08 =	0.203
2. Premium per policy		63.0	% X	1.06 =	0.668
3. Wholesale price index		11.5	% X	1.04 =	0.120
4. Rent per square foot		6.7	% X	1.02 =	0.068
	TOTAL	100.0	%	WEIGHTED CHANGE	1.059

---

*Theoretically, price changes should be weighted with consideration for the new mix of resources (current period quantity weighting). In this instance, however, we assumed that no major mix change in resources would occur.

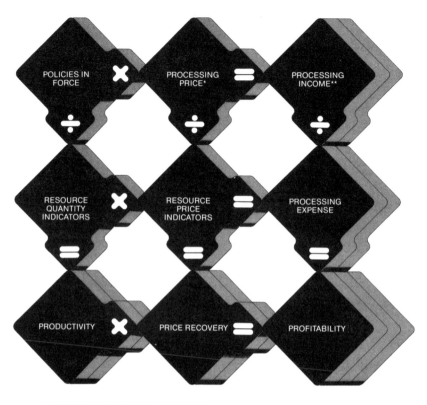

*AVERAGE PREMIUM PER POLICY — PURE PREMIUM PER POLICY
**TOTAL PREMIUM — TOTAL LOSSES INCURRED

Figure A-5

Model for Other Industries

We validated the strategic planning model outlined here for an insurance company. With only slight modifications, the same concepts can be applied to most industries.

The only difference for those industries generating tangible goods and services is their model's simplicity. The planner does not have to go through all the procedures to eliminate factors that do not affect market competition. The revenue and expense variables match the income

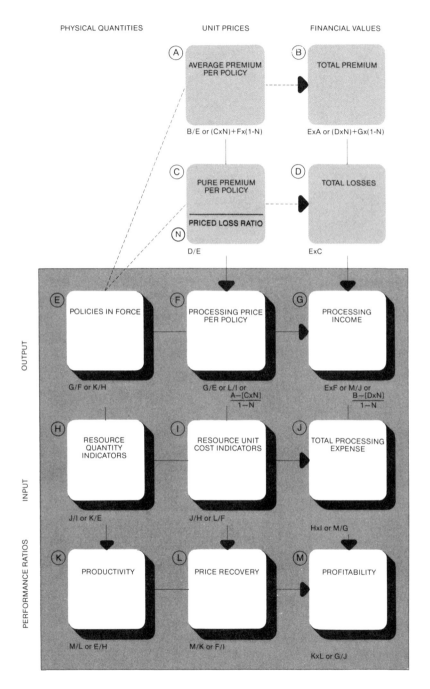

Figure A-6

211

statement. The standard weighting techniques can be used without further adjustment to product price. All the other concepts apply.

Lending and investment institutions, such as commercial banks, can also follow the standard productivity measurement model. Revenue can be the income derived from:

(i) INTEREST MARGINS This is defined as net interest income (on a taxable-equivalent basis), plus fees associated with lending and investment functions, less provisions for loan losses;

(ii) DEPOSITORY AND PAYMENT SERVICES These are fees and service charges associated with depository and payment services; and

(iii) MISCELLANEOUS SERVICES This is the value of all other income derived from miscellaneous sources such as trusts and safe-deposit rentals.

The expense items can be identified in the same manner as in the insurance model.

4. The Planning Session

We conducted our planning session with the home office officers of ABC Insurance. Before the meeting on strategic planning, the senior staff of the four geographical territories had already independently formulated their own objectives. These objectives did not go beyond the short term, however. They based their objectives on a corporate strategy to increase premium by 10 percent annually. Since the company had never conducted a planning exercise of this type, the objective of the session was simply to apply the projections to the planning model in order to analyze long-term implications.

These were the submitted objectives (expressed in change-ratios) by geographical territory:

212

Territory	Price (Average Premium Per Policy)	Quantity (Policies in Force)	Total Revenue
Northern Region	1.096	0.976	1.070
Southern Region	1.094	1.051	1.015
Eastern Region	1.132	1.014	1.148
Western Region	1.064	1.034	1.100

The price changes were actual price adjustments filed with the various state insurance commissions. The policy count changes reflected projected growth or reductions in the number of policyholders resulting from the price changes. These figures considered the different elasticities of demand for the product in different territories as a result of state insurance laws.

Using precomputed weights, we determined a weighted change for both policy count and price. The worksheets used to compute weighted policy count and price change are shown in tables A-10 and A-11 (see next page).

Table A-10
WEIGHTING POLICY COUNT CHANGE

TERREITORY		WEIGHTS % TO TOTAL PROCESSING EXPENSE	CHANGE IN POLICY COUNT	
1. *Northern Region*		*28.5* % X	*0.976* =	*.278*
2. *Southern Region*		*17.2* % X	*1.051* =	*.181*
3. *Eastern Region*		*13.5* % X	*1.014* =	*.137*
4. *Western Region*		*40.8* % X	*1.034* =	*.422*
	TOTAL	*100.0* %	WEIGHTED CHANGE	*1.018*

Table A-11
WEIGHTING PRODUCT PRICE CHANGE

TERRITORY		WEIGHTS % TO TOTAL FUTURE PREMIUM	CHANGE IN PRICE	
1. *Northern Region*		25.1 % x	1.096 =	.275
2. *Southern Region*		16.3 % x	1.094 =	.178
3. *Eastern Region*		14.5 % x	1.132 =	.164
4. *Western Region*		44.1 % x	1.064 =	.469
	TOTAL	100.0 %	WEIGHTED CHANGE	1.086

We secured projections for changes in resource prices. The human resources department developed figures projecting wage-per-hour changes over the coming year. We projected rent per square foot from a review of current leasing contracts. We also estimated the wholesale price index. We then used these figures to develop a weighted resource price change, or the inflation rate, of the resources. See table A-12.

In spite of the expected increase in policy counts, we anticipated that excess capacity in both building space and staffing would accommodate the 2-percent projected work-load gain. So, for purposes of simulation, we held employee counts, building, and equipment constant. We then developed the weighted resource quantity change as shown in table A-13.

The actuarial department provided projections on the change in average losses per policy (pure premium). We determined that this figure was a countrywide weighted change of 6.5 percent. See table A-14 on page 216.

214

Table A-12
WEIGHTING RESOURCE UNIT COST CHANGE

RESOURCE UNIT COST INDICATORS		WEIGHTS % TO TOTAL EXPENSES	RESOURCE UNIT COST CHANGE	
1. *Wage per hour*		18.8 % X	1.070 =	0.201
2. *Premium per policy*		63.0 % X	1.086 =	0.684
3. *Wholesale price index*		11.5 % X	1.075 =	0.124
4. *Rent per square foot*		6.7 % X	1.075 =	0.072
	TOTAL	100.0 %	WEIGHTED CHANGE	1.081

Table A-13
WEIGHTING RESOURCE QUANTITY CHANGE

RESOURCE QUANTITY INDICATORS		WEIGHTS % TO TOTAL EXPENSES	RESOURCE QUANTITY CHANGE	
1. *Policies in force*		74.6 % X	1.018 =	0.759
2. *Branch employee count (FTE)*		9.0 % X	1.000 =	0.090
3. *Home office employee count (FTE)*		7.9 % X	1.000 =	0.079
4. *Square feet of building space*		8.5 % X	1.000 =	0.085
	TOTAL	100.0 %	WEIGHTED CHANGE	1.013

215

Table A-14
WEIGHTING PURE PREMIUM PER POLICY CHANGE

TERRITORY		WEIGHTS % TO TOTAL PURE PREMIUM	CHANGE IN PURE PREMIUM PER POLICY	
1. *Northern Region*		24.0 % X	1.065 =	0.256
2. *Southern Region*		15.2 % X	1.062 =	0.161
3. *Eastern Region*		17.1 % X	1.070 =	0.183
4. *Western Region*		43.7 % X	1.064 =	0.465
	TOTAL	100.0 %	WEIGHTED CHANGE	1.065

In order to weight this change with respect to the total revenue, the actuarial department estimated a loss ratio of 0.73. This means that for every dollar in price, the actuarial unit expected 73 cents to be applied to benefit claims.

Applying all the data collected so far to the planning worksheet, we defined six variables. We then applied these given values to the planning worksheet shown in figure A-7. Figure A-8's worksheet (see page 218) shows the final values we computed for the rest of the variables.

The initial results revealed the following trends:

i) The company's profitability would gain 6.3 percent on an annual basis.

ii) The company's price recovery would increase 5.7 percent.

iii) The company's productivity would remain at close to the then current level.

Based on current management practices, we had every reason to believe that the company would maintain a strategy

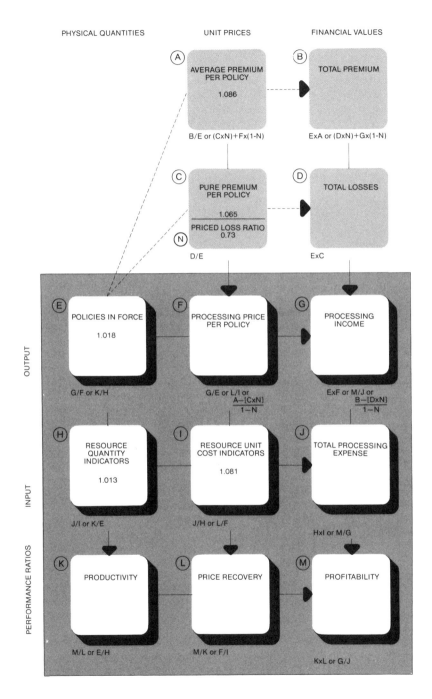

PHYSICAL QUANTITIES   UNIT PRICES   FINANCIAL VALUES

(A) AVERAGE PREMIUM PER POLICY
1.086

B/E or (CxN)+Fx(1-N)

(B) TOTAL PREMIUM

ExA or (DxN)+Gx(1-N)

(C) PURE PREMIUM PER POLICY
1.065
PRICED LOSS RATIO
0.73
(N)

D/E

(D) TOTAL LOSSES

ExC

OUTPUT

(E) POLICIES IN FORCE
1.018

G/F or K/H

(F) PROCESSING PRICE PER POLICY

G/E or L/I or $\dfrac{A-[CxN]}{1-N}$

(G) PROCESSING INCOME

ExF or M/J or $\dfrac{B-[DxN]}{1-N}$

INPUT

(H) RESOURCE QUANTITY INDICATORS
1.013

J/I or K/E

(I) RESOURCE UNIT COST INDICATORS
1.081

J/H or L/F

(J) TOTAL PROCESSING EXPENSE

HxI or M/G

PERFORMANCE RATIOS

(K) PRODUCTIVITY

M/L or E/H

(L) PRICE RECOVERY

M/K or F/I

(M) PROFITABILITY

KxL or G/J

Figure A-7

217

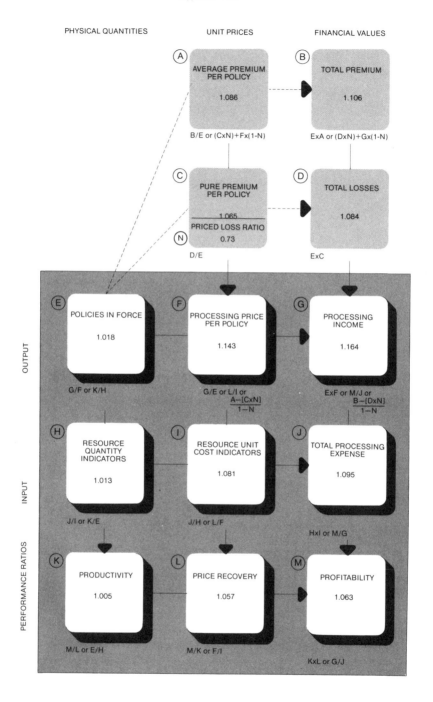

Figure A-8

characterized by the figures shown in figure A-8 over the longrun. To evaluate the implications of this trend, we analyzed the long-term position of ABC Insurance on the basis of the sector analysis chart shown in figure A-4 on page 191.

5. Analysis of ABC Insurance Co.

The planning exercise was very revealing. ABC Insurance Co. was on the borderline between sector E and sector F. Its then current strategy was to derive short-term profits from rapid increases in pricing—possibly a workable tactic for a very limited period. But if its focus on productivity were to decline, the company would possibly slowly slip within dangerous reach of sector E. At that point, there was no evidence that this would happen. ABC had always been productivity conscious.

But the company was too concerned with posting immediate profits without looking far enough ahead. Its product may have been overpriced. Already, there was evidence of tremendous excess capacity in the company's branch processing units. If new competitors were to gain hold of the market (and some were poised to do this), a decline in market share would push the company's capacity utilization down, thus dragging it down to sector E.

Given these facts, management needed to first address the productivity issue. Then it needed to set longrun productivity objectives and attain these objectives through better management of resources and increasing market share. It could achieve market penetration only by lowering the price recovery ratio; i.e., ABC needed to increase its prices to the point at which they were in line with the inflation rate of its resources. If the company was secure in expecting productivity gain, it could adopt a sector A strategy. The marginal profitability differences within the insurance industry are small, so even slight increases in productivity can make a big difference in competition.

Based on the new information displayed in figure A-8, the ABC management evaluated alternatives to the company's current strategy. An alternative plan is shown in the worksheet in figure A-9. The new, more aggressive plan is expected to result in better market penetration. These figures reflect annualized changes based on a three-year plan.

SUMMARY

Development of a strategic plan in an organization is a top-management responsibility. Without this link to the company's leader, a long-term planning session can be caught up with operational tactical decisions; there will be a shortrun mentality.

Top management should define the strategic sector that the company should be aiming for. In line with this, the company can then set profitability, productivity, and price recovery objectives.

The ideal is to conduct a planning session using a format and tools similar to those utilized by ABC Insurance Co. All of management that is affected should be involved, from the sales, marketing, and pricing officer to the processing administrator and purchasing officer. Only through such a session will the real interrelationship of one department to the other become apparent, especially if the impact of specific changes is simulated in the planning model.

As a side benefit, the more definitive objectives generated by the planning model will provide better guidelines for budget setting. One no longer needs to decide budget cuts across the board. The expectations for the management group become more realistic and their individual goals attainable. You can monitor their performance relative to the objectives through a productivity measurement system.

Finally, a strategic planning exercise of this kind forces management to look further ahead; it helps management realize that shortrun profits do not necessarily assure the attainment of a company's goal—or the assurance of its survival.

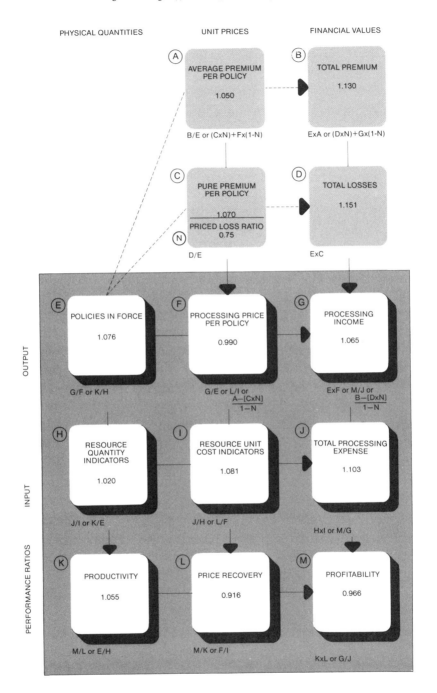

Figure A-9

APPENDIX TWO

A Summary of
*Perspectives on Productivity:
A Global View (1981)*

Perspectives on Productivity: A Global View (1981) is the most comprehensive international public opinion survey ever conducted on the subject of productivity.

Few subjects have captured the interest of the nation to a greater extent in recent years than productivity. It is fair to say that what America does to improve productivity in the next few years will affect our economic, governmental, and social relations for decades to come. Declining productivity is not simply an American problem, but one common to many nations. Yet despite considerable public discussion of this issue, little systematic information is available regarding the opinions of the public and leadership groups on what can and should be done.

Throughout the productivity debate in the United States, a recurring theme has been the need to establish a framework for a new consensus on the directions we should take to reinvigorate the economy.

SURVEY SAMPLE

Louis Harris and Associates, with the assistance of Peter Small and Associates and McBain Research, Inc., designed and conducted this study. They conducted a total of 4,711 interviews in 5 countries. Except for the leadership interviews in West Germany and Japan, which they conducted by telephone, they conducted all interviews in person.

Specifically, the sample included:

• **The adult American population.** A representative cross section of 1,201 American adults was interviewed.

• **Selected domestic leadership groups.** A total of 791 respresentatives from 8 selected groups was interviewed.

• **Employees overseas.** A representative sample of all adults regularly employed for 8 hours or more per week in Great Britain (541), West Germany (492), Australia (799), and Japan (500) was interviewed.

● **Selected leadership groups overseas.** A total of 387 representatives from 7 selected leadership groups was interviewed.

FINDINGS

1. The American Public: People throughout the United States recognize the need to improve our country's productivity. Americans know they are up against a serious problem and they are receptive to measures designed to increase the nation's productivity. They understand that improved productivity would benefit not only management and stockholders, but also employees and consumers. Clearly, the public thinks economic measures designed to stimulate investment would go a long way toward improving U.S. economic performance. The present state of public opinion offers an unusual opportunity to take new steps to improve the country's productivity.

A majority of Americans (79 percent) believes declining productivity will be a serious problem for at least the next several years. Nearly one-third takes the even stronger position that it is one of the two or three most serious problems facing the nation in the decade ahead.

The public is aware that failure to improve U.S. productivity will lead to fewer jobs (80 percent), a lower standard of living (75 percent), greater dependence on other countries (64 percent), and a decline in international respect and influence for the United States (74 percent). The American public considers these possible consequences of poor productivity both likely to occur and harmful.

The majority of U.S. employees thinks both management (60 percent) and employees (58 percent) would be among the groups benefiting most from better productivity. Almost half (48 percent) say consumers would benefit substantially.

Americans are more likely to single out the federal government (61 percent) than any other group or institution as having a major responsibility for the nation's poor productivity performance. They want less rather than more government involvement in the economy; and 45 percent think the economy would be better off with less government planning and direction than it has now. Fully 78 percent of the public believes decreased government spending would make a major contribution to improved economic growth. Majorities also feel tax cuts (58 percent), financial incentives to business for capital investment (52 percent), and financial incentives for increased consumer saving (52 percent) would have the same beneficial effect.

2. **Congress:** The mood on Capitol Hill is positive toward policy changes intended to boost productivity. One reason is that members of Congress think past Congresses bear a major responsibility for the nation's poor economic performance. Congress especially favors measures to increase capital investment by business.

Congress is even more convinced than the public of the seriousness of the nation's productivity problems. A majority (51 percent) state that declining productivity is one of the two or three most serious problems facing the nation in the 1980's.

Congress (46 percent) is also more aware than the public (23 percent) that recent U.S. productivity performance may compare unfavorably with that of most other industrial countries. Members of Congress believe to an even greater degree than the public that continued poor productivity will result in a lower standard of living (91 percent), fewer jobs (80 percent), less international respect and influence (84 percent), and greater dependence on other countries (79 percent). Congress is the only major group surveyed that feels it bears a significant responsibility for the country's productivity problems (61 percent). This admission suggests Congress is ready to move in new directions in economic policy, if it can be convinced the new policies will increase productivity.

3. **The Japanese Model:** While the United States can learn some valuable lessons from Japanese success in increasing productivity, it is not likely to follow the Japanese path to economic growth wholeheartedly. There is little enthusiasm for more government involvement in the economy, and there are

grave doubts about the active role of government in shaping economic policy. The free enterprise ethic is still very strong in the United States, and there is little support for a national economic plan or government designation of growth industries.

The public (49 percent) and Congress (56 percent) support relaxation of antitrust laws to help American companies compete more effectively in the world market. This reform could make possible formation of Japanese-style export trading companies intended to increase U.S. exports. Also in the offing might be joint ventures between existing companies to take advantage of economies of scale and to share the most up-to-date technology.

A second way the United States is likely to profit from the Japanese example is by substantially increasing capital investment by business. At present, 49 percent of American business executives, but only 23 percent of Japanese executives, report that failure to invest enough in new equipment and facilities is the factor that has done the most to inhibit growth of productivity. If, as seems likely, new economic policies channel more funds into consumer saving and capital investment by business, then the United States will have taken a major step toward the Japanese model.

There are clear limitations, however, on the application of Japanese policies in the United States. In Japan, government plays a coordinating role in the economy that would be politically impossible in the United States. While Japanese employees advocate more government planning and direction of the economy (by 51 percent to 21 percent), U.S. employees want less. Japanese business executives are about evenly divided on this issue (30 percent in favor and 33 percent opposed), whereas U.S. executives (90 percent in favor and 4 percent opposed) and Congress (63 percent in favor and 21 percent opposed) take a firm stand for less government intervention. There is little support among American leadership groups for a national economic plan to achieve economic growth. Finally, Congress (81 percent), U.S. business executives (92 percent), and even labor union leaders (67 percent) all believe government should *not* designate specific industries as growth industries deserving special assistance from government.

4. Cooperation among Management, Labor, and Government: Although the American people want less government planning and direction of the economy, they also want government to encourage greater cooperation among business, labor, special interest groups, and government itself to achieve increased productivity. The challenge for political leadership, therefore, will be to persuade these groups to look beyond their own narrow interests to the welfare of the nation as a whole. Failure to achieve such cooperation could diminish public support for policies to increase productivity.

A solid majority (59 percent) of Americans believes government encouragement of greater cooperation among business, labor, government, and special interest groups would make a major contribution to improved economic growth. The only government policy more widely thought to make a major contribution is reduced government spending.

Fifty-eight percent of the public feels that a closer working relationship between business and government to establish goals and priorities would have a major impact on economic growth. A somewhat smaller majority of the pubic believes there is presently too little cooperation between business and government.

One in four Americans thinks better relations between management and labor is one of the changes that would do the most to improve productivity in the workplace. Only financial rewards for productivity gains (30 percent) are thought to be more effective. In addition, the public considers labor unions less helpful to business growth and efficiency than they were 10 years ago (55 percent). The public is more convinced of this than Congress (47 percent), business executives (38 percent), or labor leaders themselves (15 percent). Finally, Americans feel there is generally too little cooperation between business and labor unions (52 percent).

5. American Employees: American employees are willing to make certain important sacrifices of their workplace prerogatives to achieve higher productivity. They are very reluctant, however, to accept reductions in their own standard of living. If a national consensus for higher productivity is to be achieved and successfully maintained, government and business leaders must not create the impression that they are demanding economic sacrifices from the ordinary citizen alone.

American employees (61 percent) are more convinced of the general principle that sacrifices in the nation's standard of living and quality-of-life are necessary to achieve an acceptable level of economic growth than U.S. business executives (51 percent), Congress (46 percent), or labor leaders (44 percent). They believe in the need for sacrifice as much as employees in Britain (58 percent) and West Germany (60 percent), and more than employees in Australia (43 percent) and Japan (24 percent).

Employees in the United States go on to say that if they were convinced that their sacrifices would provide money needed for investment to achieve economic growth, they would be willing to be reassigned to work wherever help was needed in their company (74 percent) and have their salaries linked to higher personal productivity (63 percent). Their willingness to lend a hand wherever help is needed in their company is especially important. It suggests employees are more prepared to be flexible in the interest of overall company efficiency than is often believed. Sacrifices in the workplace most employees are *not* personally willing to make include taking a cut in hours and corresponding pay (66 vs. 31 percent), being retrained for another job at a lesser salary (78 vs. 18 percent), and taking a substantial salary cut with no cut in hours (82 vs. 15 percent). In addition, a majority of employees say they would be unwilling to pay higher taxes (66 vs. 30 percent) or accept higher levels of unemployment (79 vs. 17 percent) to increase investment.

6. American Labor Leaders: Labor leaders seem somewhat out of touch with the political climate in Congress and the country at large regarding U.S. productivity and what should be done to improve it. In addition, both the public and employees themselves feel labor unions bear a major responsibility for the nation's productivity problems.

229

Labor leaders view U.S. productivity problems as much less serious than the public or Congress. Only 20 percent of labor leaders say declining productivity is one of the two or three most serious problems facing the nation in the 1980's, compared with 31 percent of the public and 51 percent of Congress. In line with this view, labor leaders are somewhat less concerned about whether the country will do what is necessary to improve its economic performance: 28 percent are very confident the needed steps will be taken, versus 20 percent of the public and 14 percent of Congress.

Labor does not agree with Congress and business executives on whether government should replace detailed regulations for business with general goals and standards. Only 33 percent of labor leaders, versus 75 percent of Congress and 92 percent of business leaders, favor this change. Labor also does not see eye to eye with Congress and the public on other specific policy issues.

- Thirty-eight percent, compared with 56 percent of Congress and 49 percent of the public, support relaxation of antitrust laws to enable U.S. companies to compete more effectively overseas

- Forty-three percent, as against 57 percent of Congress and 58 percent of the public, think tax cuts could make a major contribution to improved economic growth.

Furthermore, labor leaders differ from the public and Congress on how much unions have contributed to productivity problems. Thirty-six percent of these leaders say unions bear a major responsibility for the country's productivity not being better than it is, compared with 52 percent of the public, 56 percent of employees, and 79 percent of Congress. Only 15 percent of labor leaders believe unions do less than they did 10 years ago to help business grow and become more efficient. Majorities of the public (55 percent), employees (56 percent), and Congress (47 percent) take this position.

7. Government Bailouts: Companies in financial trouble that approach the government for emergency assistance will have to make a strong case for themselves in the future if their appeals are to be successful. On the other hand, preservation of existing jobs and the importance of certain industries to the national defense are still effective arguments for government bailouts.

By a plurality, but not a majority (48 percent in favor; 33 percent opposed), the public thinks major companies in severe financial trouble should be left to sink or swim on their own instead of being bailed out by government. Another 15 percent thinks each case should be decided on its own merits.

The Congress is more decisive; it opposes bailouts by a much greater margin than the public (69 percent). The only major leadership group not completely opposed to bailouts is labor, of whom only a plurality (44 percent) says companies should sink or swim on their own.

If companies are to be bailed out, important conditions may be attached. The danger that employees could perceive the sacrifices required of different groups as inequitable can be seen in attitudes regarding these conditions. Approximately equal proportions of the public believe bailouts should occur only if workers' wages and benefits are reduced in the companies concerned and only if top management in those companies is completely replaced. Business executives, on the other hand, favor sacrifice by workers (69 percent) much more than sacrifice by management (31 percent) in this situation. Members of Congress have similar attitudes: 47 percent favor worker sacrifice and 21 percent, management replacement. From an international perspective, U.S. business leaders are less even-handed on this issue than business leaders in Britain or Australia. British leaders show fairly equal support for sacrifice by workers (40 percent) and management (37 percent), as do Australian leaders (by 37 percent and 42 percent, respectively).

Arguments against bailouts on the grounds that they amount to subsidizing inefficiency must confront the public's strong desire to preserve existing jobs. Of a number of sacrifices the country might make to achieve better economic growth, the one least acceptable to the public and Congress is higher levels of unemployment. In addition, the public reverses its position on bailouts when the companies in question are important to the national defense. Three-quarters of the public and just over half of the Congress support government aid for failing companies that are important to U.S. security.

8. Industrial and Service-Sector Executives in America: Executives of industrial companies and service-sector companies in the United States hold fairly similar views on productivity. There are, however, several differences worth noting. First, executives of industrial companies are more prone to think U.S. productivity problems are serious. Second, they are more likely than service-sector executives to believe that business leaders are partly responsible for the problem and that, by adopting a long-term outlook, executives would increase productivity substantially. Finally, they put less emphasis on the human factor in workplace productivity and more emphasis on capital equipment than do executives in service-sector companies.

Sixty percent of industrial executives, versus 52 percent of service-sector executives, say declining productivity is one of the two or three most serious problems facing the nation. Likewise, 49 percent of industrial executives versus 40 percent of service-sector executives believe U.S. economic performance is worse than performance in most other industrial countries.

Executives in industrial companies (41 percent) are more likely than those in service-sector companies (31 percent) to concede that large corporations bear a major responsibility for U.S. productivity not being better than it is. Twenty-nine percent of industrial executives, compared with 17 percent of service-sector executives, say a short-term outlook on the part of business management has contributed a great deal to U.S. economic problems. Almost three in four industrial executives (74 percent) think that less emphasis by business on short-term profits, coupled with a long-term outlook, would make a major contribution to economic growth. Fewer service-sector executives (66 percent) hold this view.

Industrial executives think that, in the workplace, use of better equipment or tools (70 percent) would do the most to improve productivity, while service-sector executives also stress better equipment (60 percent). They attach even more importance to employees getting financial rewards for productivity gains (67 percent vs. 60 percent for industrial executives). Bonuses for employees that rise or fall depending on the company's profits also receive greater emphasis from service-sector executives (38 percent vs. 26 percent for their industrial counterparts).

9. **Ways To Improve Productivity:** There is widespread support for two different approaches to improving productivity: steps to increase investment and steps to increase employee motivation. Employees and business executives in the United States agree that the improvements in the workplace that would do the most to increase productivity are employees getting financial rewards for productivity gains, the use of better equipment or tools, and better management-labor relations. But management might also take note of other changes employees think would contribute almost as much to increased productivity: employees having more say in decisions that affect them, more job security, and better fringe benefits.

American business executives believe use of better equipment or tools (65 percent), employees receiving financial rewards for productivity gains (63 percent), and better relations between management and labor (44 percent) would do much more than other workplace improvements to increase productivity.

While employees agree these improvements are among the most important, they focus less exclusively on these areas than executives. Unlike business leaders, many employees think having more say in decisions that affect them (22 percent), more job security (21 percent), and better fringe benefits (20 percent) are among the most important stimulants to greater productivity in the workplace.

10. **A New Consensus:** The survey points to the need for a new consensus to improve productivity performance in the United States. International comparisons strongly suggest cooperation among management, labor, and government is a major factor in increasing productivity in West Germany and Japan.

The attitudes of Japanese and West German employees and business executives toward cooperation among the principal economic institutions in the society generally reflect greater satisfaction with the degree of cooperation achieved than the attitudes of American and British employees and business leaders. The same pattern can be seen in views on government planning and direction for the economy. Those who believe in the benefits of an adversary relationship—for example, between government and business or between labor and management—will find little support in this survey.

Japanese employees are less likely than those in the other countries surveyed to say there is too little cooperation between government and business (21 percent). By contrast, in the United States and Britain, a majority of employees thinks there is too much cooperation between government and business. Business leaders in the United States and Britain are more likely to say too little cooperation exists between government and business than are executives in West Germany and Japan.

When it comes to cooperation between business and labor unions, the Japanese stand out sharply from other nations. Only 36 percent of Japanese employees versus a majority in the United States (53 percent) and Britain (62 percent) think there is too little cooperation between business and labor in their country. A tiny 15 percent of Japanese business leaders, as opposed to 61 percent of U.S. business leaders and 71 percent of British business leaders, believe business and labor unions don't cooperate enough with one another. Furthermore, half of the Japanese business leaders surveyed believe that in the last 10 years, labor unions in their country have become more helpful in assisting business to grow and become more efficient. This opinion is in sharp contrast to those held by executives in the United States and Britain, who generally feel unions have become less helpful to the business community.

The similarity of American views to British rather than Japanese attitudes can also be seen on the question of whether there should be more or less government planning and direction for the economy. Pluralities of American (46 percent) and

British (42 percent) employees opt for less government planning and direction. In Japan, only one in five employees wants less, and a slim majority actually wants more.

11. Business Executives Around the World: American business executives differ markedly from those in other countries on several key questions. First, they are much more hostile to the goals of the environmental movement and to government environmental policies than business executives in Britain and Australia. Second, they are generally more likely than their British and Australian counterparts to accept policies with a potential for social costs—such as pollution, unemployment, and poverty—in order to increase capital investment. Finally, they are far readier than business leaders in Britain, West Germany, Australia, or Japan to believe the economy would perform better with less government planning and direction.

A 57-percent majority of American business executives believes relaxation of environmental and safety regulations would make a major contribution to improved economic growth. British (7 percent) and Australian (13 percent) business executives part company with their U.S. counterparts on this issue. These findings suggest American business leaders see productivity and environmental protection as conflicting rather than complementary goals.

American business executives also differ sharply from British and Australian business leaders in their willingness to accept higher levels of air and water pollution to achieve better economic growth. Two in three (67 percent) U.S. business executives say they would accept such a trade-off, compared with 28 percent in Britain and 23 percent in Australia.

Almost three-quarters (73 percent) of U.S. business leaders would be willing to accept less government spending for the poor and other disadvantaged groups if they were convinced it would increase capital investment. By comparison, only 22 percent of British executives and 12 percent of Australian executives would be willing to make this trade-off. With the same proviso, 70 percent of U.S. business executives, versus 49 percent of executives in Britain and 33 percent of executives in

Australia, would be willing to accept higher levels of unemployment. An overwhelming 93 percent of American executives would be willing to accept less government spending for health and education, versus 62 percent in Britain and 66 percent in Australia.

Nine in 10 U.S. executives believe the economy would perform better with less government planning and direction. In contrast, 50 percent of British executives, 49 percent of Australian executives, 39 percent of West German executives, and only 33 percent of Japanese executives take this position.

For a complimentary copy of the full study *Perspectives on Productivity: A Global View (1981),* direct your requests to:

Creative Management Alternatives, Inc.*

1800 North Point Drive

Stevens Point, WI 54481

* A Sentry Enterprise.

Index

238